Our Discovery Island

5

T0383554

STUDENT BOOK

Ice Island

John Wiltshier • José Luis Morales
Series Advisor: David Nunan

Series Consultants:
Hilda Martínez • Xóchitl Arvizu

Advisory Board:
Tim Budden • Tina Chen • Betty Deng
Aaron Jolly • Dr. Nam-Joon Kang
Dr. Wonkey Lee • Wenxin Liang
Ann Mayeda • Wade O. Nichols
Jamie Zhang

Pearson Education Limited
Edinburgh Gate
Harlow
Essex CM20 2JE
England
and Associated Companies throughout the world.

Our Discovery Island ™

www.ourdiscoveryisland.com

© Pearson Education Limited 2012

The *Our Discovery Island* series is an independent educational course published by Pearson Education Limited and is not affiliated with, or authorized, sponsored, or otherwise approved by Discovery Communications LLC or Discovery Education, Inc.

Based on the work of Fiona Beddall

The rights of John Wiltshier, José Luis Morales, and Fiona Beddall to be identified as authors of this work have been asserted by them in accordance with the Copyright, Designs and Patents Act 1988.

Stories on pages 6–7, 18, 30, 42, 54, 66, 78, 90, and 102 by Steve Elsworth and Jim Rose. The rights of Steve Elsworth and Jim Rose to be identified as authors of this work have been asserted by them in accordance with the Copyright, Designs and Patents Act 1988.

First published 2012
Fifteenth impression 2022

ISBN: 978-1-4479-0065-8

Set in Longman English 12.5/15pt
Printed in Slovakia by Neografia

Illustrators: Charlotte Alder (The Bright Agency), Fred Blunt, Lawrence Christmas, Leo Cultura, Mark Draisey, John Martz, Simone Massoni (Advocate Art), Rob McClurkan (Beehive Illustration), Ken Mok, Dickie Seto, and Olimpia Wong

Picture Credits: The Publishers would like to thank the following for their kind permission to reproduce their photographs: (Key: b-bottom; c-centre; l-left; r-right; t-top) Alamy Images: Rex Allen 70bl, Arcticphoto 53r, Aurora Photos 71b, Blend Images 16t, dbimages 47cl, Johnny Greig Portraits 41tr, Images of Africa Photobank 94tr, Johner Images 47tr, MBI 16b, moodboard 65 (b), Picture Partners 47tl, Robert Harding Picture Library Ltd 49c, Helen Sessions 82 (a), shinypix 101c, Stock Connection Distribution 22cr, Striking Images 82 (b), Studioshots 82 (c), Peter Titmuss 100t, Jim West 40r, Janine Wiedel Photolibrary 89t; Art Directors and TRIP Photo Library: Tibor Bognar 70tl, Helene Rogers 82 (e), 82t (d), 82b (d); Asian Disc Photos: 20; Bridgeman Art Library Ltd: The Barnes Foundation, Merion, Pennsylvania, USA 17l; Trevor Clifford: 26; Corbis: Christophe Boisvieux 47cr, Kevin Dodge 23tl, Patrik Giardino 89b, Jon Hicks 64b, Wolfgang Kaehler 53l, Johannes Kroemer 46br, Francis G. Mayer 17r, Will & Deni McIntyre 95tr, Tomas Rodriguez 64t; FLPA Images of Nature: Michael & Patricia Fogden / Minden Pictures 49r, Dietmar Nill / Minden Pictures 88 (b); Getty Images: blue jean images 23cr, Matt Cardy 46bl, Kevin Cooley / Taxi 76, Erin Patrice O'Brien / Taxi 40l; iStockphoto: Ron Bailey 100tc, Michael Braun 94tl, Sebastian Kopp 29c, Huchen Lu 23tr, Irina Shoyhet 46cl; Kobal Collection Ltd: DREAMWORKS / PARAMOUNT 41cr, Offspring Entertainment 65 (c); Evans Kweyu: 95cl; Pearson Education Ltd: Sophie Bluy 11, Trevor Clifford 34t, 58t, 106/1, Image Source Ltd 19, Rob Judges 15, Studio 8 52, 59; Photolibrary.com: B2M Productions 14, GARDEL Bertrand / Hemis 40cl, Jaume Gual / age fotostock , 29l, Luca Invernizzi Tettoni / Tips Italia 47bl, Eduardo M Rivero / age fotostock , 49l, Pixtal Images 101b, J S Sira / Garden Picture Library 71t; Press Association Images: AP / Eckehard Schulz 101t, Ross D. Franklin / AP 46tr, Johanna Hanno / Scanpix 94br; Rex Features: Steve Hill 22l, WestEnd61 41 (b); Shutterstock.com: 300dpi 61b (e), 61t (e), Aaron Amat 61b (b), Apollofoto 97/4, Yuri Arcurs 12/6, 62 (a), ArtmannWitte 55tl, Jeff Banke 106/2, Nikola Bilic 62 (e), Goran Bogicevic 57 (6b), Bomshtein 61b (h), Dan Breckwoldt 88 (c), cabania 27l, Carlos Caetano 57 (4b), Ilker Canikligil 62 (d), Corepics 88 (a), Cristi180884 63/2, David Davis 97/3, djem 40cr, DNF-Style Photography 62 (b), Michelle Donahue Hillison 100b, Kevin Eaves 51 (b), Junial Enterprises 38r, Iakov Filimonov 48 (m), Gelpi 39, 43r, GG Pro Photo 87, Goldencow Images 27t, granata1111 48 (k), Péter Gudella 61b (f), Image Focus 57 (2a), Irafael 57 (1b), Rafa Irusta 61t (i), Jaggat 38l, jeka84 61b (a), Judex 57 (5a), Michael Jung 106/3, Olga Kadroff 61b (g), Karkas 61t (c), Kayros Studio 61t (f), Simon Krzic 55b, Kurhan 25b, Lana Langlois 43l, RJ Lerich 34 (b), 58cr, Mamahoohooba 51 (a), Mates 63/1, Dudarev Mikhail 51 (d), Mikhail 61b (d), Karam Miri 63/4, Monkey Business Images 79, 88b, Naluwan 51bc, 97/6, 106/4, Nic Neish 97/2, Olinchuk 63/3, Oliveromg 34 (d), 58c, Ostill 34 (c), 58l, Pakhnyushcha 51 (c), Paulaphoto 27br, 97/5, Denis Pepin 41 (d), PhotoNAN 61t (d), Andrejs Pidjass 12/8, Tatiana Popova 61t (g), Glenda M. Powers 25t, Rachael Russell 57 (3a), Aliaksei Sabelnikau 51br, saiko3p 61t (h), Brad Sauter 12/2, Sculpies 57 (5b), Semisatch 61b (c), Sergios 34 (a), 58br, 106/5, SergiyN 31, 106/6, sliper84 57 (3b), Emjay Smith 57 (6a), Brigida Soriano 57 (4a), Perov Stanislav 62 (f), Jason Stitt 12/1, 12/3, Svemir 41 (a), Taelove7 61t (b), Titelio 62 (c), Tomasz Trojanowski 37, 107, upthebanner 57 (1a), Goncalo Veloso de Figueiredo 65/2, vgstudio 12/5, Danny Warren 65 (a), wow 55tr, Vladimir Wrangel 51 (e), Yabu 57 (2b), Lisa F. Young 12/4, 92t, 92b, Feng Yu 61t (a), Arman Zhenikeyev 97/1; Thinkstock: 29r, 65/1, 65/3, 94bl, BananaStock 89c, Creatas Images 70br, Goodshoot 71c, Pixland 41 (c), and Stockbyte 22tr.

All other images © Pearson Education Limited

Contents

Scope and sequence

Welcome

Vocabulary	**Time:** two days ago, yesterday, today, tomorrow
Structures	Two days ago was Saturday. I played tennis on Monday morning. He/She danced at the party on Friday evening. They went to the movies on Saturday afternoon.

1 Friends

Vocabulary	**Physical appearance:** dark hair, light hair, spiky hair, bald, handsome, beautiful, good-looking, cute **Adjectives to describe personality:** bossy, kind, sporty, lazy, clever, shy, talkative, helpful, friendly, hard-working	**Cross-curricular:** **Art:** Warm and cool colors **Values:** Help your friends in class.
Structures	What does he/she look like? He's/She's good-looking. He/She has straight, dark hair and brown eyes. What do they look like? They're tall and good-looking. They have short, light hair and blue eyes. He/She doesn't have light hair. They don't have light hair. What's he/she like? He's/She's sporty and he's/she's clever. He's/She's bossy but hard-working. I like him/her because he's/she's kind.	

2 My life

Vocabulary	**Daily activities:** brush my teeth, make my bed, wash my face, clean my room, do my homework, meet my friends, study before a test, take notes in class, take out the garbage, be on time **Adverbs of frequency:** never, sometimes, usually, often, always	**Cross-curricular:** **Social science:** Being healthy **Values:** Giving is great.
Structures	You must brush your teeth. *(Order)* You should brush your teeth. *(Advice)* I never brush my teeth. / He sometimes brushes his teeth. / She usually brushes her teeth. / They often brush their teeth. / We always brush our teeth.	

3 Free time

Vocabulary	**Activities and hobbies:** hitting, kicking, throwing, catching, diving, going shopping, telling jokes, reading poetry, trampolining, playing video games, playing chess, playing the drums, acting, singing in a choir, running races, singing karaoke, in-line skating	**Cross-curricular:** **Music:** Musical instruments **Values:** Try new things. Have a hobby.
Structures	What's he/she good at? He/She's good at hitting. What are they good at? They're good at hitting. He/She isn't good at catching. / They aren't good at catching. What does he/she like/love doing? He/She likes/loves going shopping. What were you doing yesterday at 7:00? I was going to school. What was he/she doing yesterday at 7:00? He/She was going to school. What were they doing yesterday at 7:00? They were going to school. Were you going to school? Yes, I was. / No, I wasn't. Was he/she going to school? Yes, he/she was. / No, he/she wasn't. Were they going to school? Yes, they were. / No, they weren't.	

4 Around the world

Vocabulary	**Countries:** China, Korea, Japan, Australia, the United States, Mexico, Colombia, Brazil, Argentina, the United Kingdom, Spain, Italy, Egypt, India **Places:** pyramid, statue, cave, volcano, city, town, farm, factory, castle
Structures	There's a rain forest in Brazil. / There isn't a rain forest in Korea. There are some penguins in Argentina. / There aren't any penguins in Italy. Is there a pyramid in the city? Yes, there is. / No, there isn't. Are there any beaches in Australia? Yes, there are some beautiful beaches in Australia. Are there any volcanoes in the United Kingdom? No, there aren't.

Cross-curricular:
Geography: Seasons

Values: Teamwork is important.

5 Shopping

Vocabulary	**Clothing and accessories:** jacket, swimsuit, watch, bracelet, wallet, handbag, umbrella, gloves, sunglasses **Adjectives to describe clothing and accessories:** tight, baggy, cheap, expensive, old-fashioned, modern
Structures	How much is this/that jacket? It's ninety dollars and fifty cents. How much are these/those sunglasses? They're thirty dollars. Whose watch is this? It's Maddy's/mine/yours/his/hers. Whose pens are these? They're Dan's/mine/yours/his/hers.

Cross-curricular:
Science:
Properties of materials

Values: Dress correctly for each occasion.

6 Party time

Vocabulary	**Irregular past tense verbs:** make/made, have/had, come/came, give/gave, get/got, sing/sang, bring/brought, meet/met, eat/ate, see/saw **Ordinal numbers:** first, second, third, fourth, fifth, sixth, seventh, eighth, ninth, tenth, eleventh, twelfth, thirteenth, fourteenth, fifteenth, sixteenth, seventeenth, eighteenth, nineteenth, twentieth, twenty-first
Structures	I made a cake. / I didn't make a cake. Where did you go? I went to Ghana. When did you go to Ghana? I went on August 1st. What did you see? I saw giant butterflies.

Cross-curricular:
History: The first Thanksgiving

Values: Be a creative problem solver.

7 School

Vocabulary	**Adjectives:** interesting, boring, exciting, scary, funny, difficult, easy, romantic **School subjects:** computer science, math, geography, science, history, art, music, P.E.
Structures	Was it interesting? Yes, it was. / No, it wasn't. Was there an alien in it? Yes, there was. / No, there wasn't. Were there any exciting stories? Yes, there were. / No, there weren't. Did you have computer science on Tuesday? Yes, I did. / No, I didn't. Was math difficult? Yes, it was. / No, it wasn't. It was easy.

Cross-curricular:
Social science:
Life experiences

Values: Learn about your older family members' youth.

8 Entertainment

Vocabulary	**Nationalities:** Chinese, Korean, Japanese, Australian, American, Mexican, Colombian, Brazilian, Argentinian, British, Spanish, Italian, Egyptian, Indian **Occupations:** cowboy, king, queen, scientist, spy, soldier, sailor, waiter, actor, musician
Structures	Is he/she from the United States? Yes, he/she is. / No, he/she isn't. Where's he/she from? He's/She's from Argentina. He's/She's Argentinian. Where are they from? They're from Australia. They're Australian. He's a cowboy. He likes playing the guitar. He's a cowboy who likes playing the guitar. It's an American movie. It's very famous. It's an American movie that's very famous.

Cross-curricular:
Technology:
Video games

Values: Be a good role model for others.

Welcome

2 (A:03) **Listen and number.**

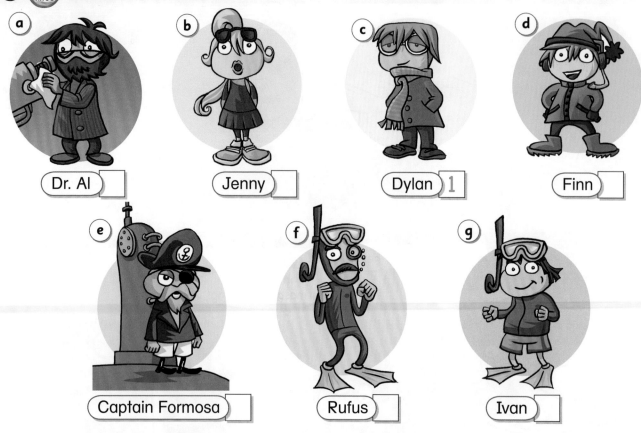

Dr. Al ☐ Jenny ☐ Dylan [1] Finn ☐

Captain Formosa ☐ Rufus ☐ Ivan ☐

3 (A:03) **Listen again and write.**

backpack   diving   penguins   rock climbing   running   stars   think

1 This is _____Dylan_____. He likes to _____ and solve problems.

2 This is _____. She likes adventure and has a _____ full of useful things.

3 This is _____. He likes skiing, snowboarding, and _____.

4 This is _____. He likes watching the _____ and planets.

5 This is _____. He likes _____ and he lives in an old submarine.

6 This is _____. He likes _____ and he is strong.

7 This is _____. He likes _____ and wants to find the treasure.

4  **Listen and match.**

(1) gets up   (3) cleans his room   (5) goes swimming
    (2) eats lunch   (4) meets friends

5 **Write.**

a She is _____ .

b He is _____ .

c _____

d _____

e _____

f _____

g _____

h _____ a rocket.

6 Look at Jenny's diary for last week and write.

A:05 **LOOK!**

I played tennis on Monday morning.

He/She danced at the party on Friday evening.

They went to the movies on Saturday afternoon.

	Monday	Tuesday	Wednesday	Thursday	Friday
morning	study	study	study	study with Dylan	study
afternoon	study	play computer games	play tennis with Finn	practice the piano	study
evening	practice the piano	watch TV	listen to music	go to the movies	watch TV

1 She _____practiced_____ the piano on Monday evening and Thursday afternoon.

2 She _____ computer games on Tuesday afternoon.

3 She _____ to music on Wednesday evening.

4 She _____ with Dylan on Thursday morning.

5 She _____ to the movies on Thursday evening.

6 She _____ TV on Friday evening.

TIP!

listen	listened
play	played
practice	practiced
study	studied
watch	watched
go	went

See more on p. 116.

7 A:06 **Listen and number. Then write.**

a

b

c

d

e

f

a She _____ her room.

b They _____ badminton.

c They _____ TV.

d She _____ the piano.

e He _____ to school.

f They _____ at school.

8 **A:07** **Listen and say.**

two days ago	yesterday	today	tomorrow
Saturday	Sunday	Monday	Tuesday

Now

9 **A:08** **Listen and read.**

Now it's 10 o'clock.
Today is Monday.
Tomorrow is Tuesday.

Yesterday was Sunday.
Two days ago was Saturday.

10 **Write.**

Now it's 3 o'clock.

1 Now it's _____.

2 Today is _____.

3 Tomorrow is _____.

4 Yesterday was _____.

5 Two days ago was _____.

11 **A:09** **Listen and match. Then write.**

(two weeks ago)   (three years ago)   (yesterday)   (two days ago)

1 I _____ that _____.

2 I _____.

3 We _____.

4 I _____.

12 **Talk about yourself.**

I walked to school yesterday.

1 Friends

1 A:10 **Listen and read. Who lives at number 12?**

1
There's a new family at number 12!

What do they look like?

The dad is tall and bald. There's a girl, too. She has curly, blond hair.

2
Hi. I'm Emma. Can I help?

Thanks! I'm Maddy.

3
Is that your cat?

What does it look like?

It has spiky, red hair.

4
Spiky, red hair? My cat, Kipper, doesn't have red hair. He's black and white.

Oh, no! Red paint!

2 A:11 **Listen and say.**

1 dark hair
2 light hair
3 spiky hair
4 bald
5 handsome
6 beautiful
7 good-looking
8 cute

3 A:12 **Who's who? Listen and number using the words in Activity 2.**

a brother ☐   b Jack ☐   c aunt ☐   d Grandpa ☐

e uncle ☐   f sister ☐   g best friend ☐ ☐

Physical appearance

LOOK! A:13

What does he/she look like?	He's/She's good-looking. He/She has straight, dark hair and brown eyes.
What do they look like?	They're tall and good-looking. They have short, light hair and blue eyes.

He/She doesn't have light hair.
They don't have light hair.

4 A:14 **Listen and read. Then look and say the names.**

1 She has light hair and blue eyes.
2 He has spiky hair and brown eyes.
3 She has straight hair and glasses.
4 He has brown hair and green eyes.
5 They have brown hair.

Maddy

Emma

Robbie

Dan

5 **Ask and answer. True or False?**

A: What does Maddy look like?
B: She has dark hair.
A: False! She has light hair.

6 **Ask and answer.**

A: He.
B: What does he look like?
A: He has long hair and a beard. He doesn't have a mustache.
B: He's number 2!

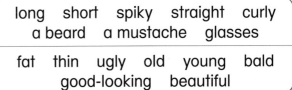

long   short   spiky   straight   curly a beard   a mustache   glasses
fat   thin   ugly   old   young   bald good-looking   beautiful

7 A:15 **Listen and say.**

a bossy

b kind

c sporty

d lazy

e clever

f shy

g talkative

h helpful

i friendly

j hard-working

8 A:16-17 **Listen to the song and write.**

SONG

You have me, and I have you.
You help, you listen, and I do, too.
We're friends. We're friends.

Ben's _____ at home,

He's _____ at school.

But he's _____ and _____,

And very cool.

We're friends. We're friends.

Jim's sometimes _____,

But I don't mind.

I like him, because he's _____.

We're friends. We're friends.
We're friends. We're friends.

9 **Look at Activity 8 and write.**

1 What's Ben like?   Ben is _____ and _____.

He's _____ and _____, too.

2 What's Jim like?   Jim is _____ but _____.

10  **Listen and match. Then ask and answer.**

A:19

LOOK!

A:18

What's he/she like?

He's/She's sporty and he's/she's clever.

He's/She's bossy but hard-working.

I like him/her because he's/she's kind.

1 Dan **2** Emma **3** Maddy **4** Robbie

a sporty / bossy   **b** kind / funny

c sporty / clever   **d** clever / lazy

What's Maddy like?

She's clever but lazy.

11  **Circle.**

1 I like my new teacher (because / but) she isn't bossy.

2 He's sporty (and / but) clever. Perfect combination!

3 My best friend is talkative (and / but) funny. She makes me laugh!

4 She gets good grades (because / but) she's very hard-working.

5 He's lazy at home (but / and) he's hard-working in class. Strange!

6 He doesn't have many friends (because / but) he's very shy. Let's talk to him!

12 **Write about two people in your family. Then tell a friend.**

1 _____

   _____

2 _____

   _____

I like my grandma because she isn't bossy. She's funny and kind.

13 A:20 **Read. Is Seb happy?**

The Torres family

Seb

From: seb@yoohoo.com
To: matt@gogomail.com
Subject: Spain!

Hi Matt,

I'm having a great time here in Spain. I'm staying with the Torres family this summer. They have a beautiful home in Madrid. It's very nice here!

Carlos is twelve. He's shy but he's very kind. He's smart, too. My Spanish isn't very good but he speaks great English! His grandma lives in Los Angeles and she speaks English with Carlos.

He has two sisters, Nerea and Lucia. Nerea is eighteen. She has beautiful, black hair and she's very sporty. She isn't at home this week because she's playing in a big tennis competition. Lucia is nine. She's funny but she's very bossy. She wants to play games all the time!

See you soon,

Seb

14 **Circle T = True or F = False.**

1 Seb is in Spain. T / F 2 Seb is staying in a nice home. T / F

3 Carlos is smart. T / F 4 Nerea likes sport. T / F

5 Carlos has a shy sister. T / F

15 **Write Seb's conversation with his mom. Then role-play with a friend.**

Are you having a good time? I'm having a great time!

Seb's mom Seb

1 Are you having a good time? _____

2 What's Carlos like? _____

3 What does he look like? _____

4 Does he have a brother or sister? _____

5 What are they like? _____

16 **Look and read. Do you like the pictures? Why?**

A

This picture is by Auguste Renoir. It is in warm colors. Renoir is an artist from France. He lived from 1841 to 1919.

B

17 **Look and say.**

It's Picture A!

1 This picture has a lot of yellow and red.
2 This picture has a lot of green and white.
3 This picture has cool colors.
4 This picture has warm colors.

This picture is by Vincent van Gogh. It is in cool colors. Van Gogh is an artist from the Netherlands. He lived from 1853 to 1890.

18 **Imagine and answer the questions. Then share with a friend.**

THINK!

What colors make you feel happy?
What colors make you feel sad?

1 What time of day is it in Picture A?
2 How do the girls in Picture A feel?
3 How does Picture A make you feel?
4 How does Picture B make you feel?
5 How do you think Van Gogh felt when he painted Picture B?

MINI-**PROJECT**
Find a painting you like and write about it.

19 A:22 **Listen and read.**

20 **How does Dylan know what the message is? Discuss your answers.**

 **21** **Write.**

1 Who has an emergency? _____

2 What does Captain Formosa want? _____

3 Where's Captain Formosa? _____

4 What does he look like? What's he like? _____

5 Is he dancing? _____

6 Are Finn, Dylan, and Jenny helpful? _____

 22 **Role-play the story.**

 **VALUES**

Help your friends in class.

23 **Read and write 1 to 5**
(1 = not important, 5 = very important).
Then compare with a friend.

How can you help?	You	Your friend
1 Listen when your friends speak.		
2 Be helpful. Share your things.		
3 Be polite. Let others speak.		
4 Be friendly. Invite shy friends to work with you.		
5 Offer: "Can I help you?"		

Listen when your friends speak. 5.

Be helpful. Share your things. 4.

HOME-SCHOOL LINK

Tell your family how you helped **PARENT** your friends in class today.

24 Create a new character.

1 Circle.

My new
character is ....

thin fat ugly
handsome happy
beautiful bald
scary sporty
good-looking short tall

2 Write.
My new character has .... (thin, long, short, pink, etc.)

_____ _____ hair

a _____ body   _____ legs

a _____ head   _____ arms

a _____ face   _____ eyes

a _____ mouth   _____ ears

3 Draw. Then tell a friend.

4 Listen to your friend. Draw his/her new character.

5 Tell the class about your character. What is it like?

helpful bossy clever lazy
sporty shy friendly kind
funny talkative hard-working

My new character is tall and handsome. He has short, dark hair and green eyes. He's shy but helpful.

25 **Listen and check (✓), or write.**

1

2

3

4

5 What does her sister look like?

She _____ long hair and _____.

6 What does their new teacher look like?

He _____ tall and _____.

26 **Write. Then match.**

(clever   are   cute   friendly   look   do)

1 Is your sister _____?

2 What _____ rabbits _____ like?

3 My dog is _____!

4 My friends _____ sporty and _____.

a They like tennis and math.

b Yes, she's beautiful.

c He likes playing with me.

d They have long ears and round tails.

I CAN
I can answer questions about what people look like.
I can talk about the personalities of my friends and family.

 TEACHER

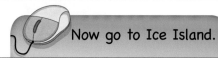 Now go to Ice Island.

Wider world 1
Families of the world

1 A:24 **Listen and read. Are the families big or small?**

2 **Number the photos.**

① Kyle's blog ✕

In the United Kingdom, we have a lot of different families—some are big and some are small. My family is quite big now. My mom has a new husband and he's great. He's very clever and he helps me with my homework. He has two sons, so now I have two brothers. We play soccer together every Saturday. We argue but, after five minutes, it's all OK! They're my brothers and my good friends.

Kyle, 12, United Kingdom

② Lang's blog ✕

A lot of families here in China have only one child. My friends and I don't have brothers or sisters but we aren't sad. Brothers and sisters can be bossy! We can do what we want. We have a good life and we have very good friends. I live with my mom and dad, and my grandma and grandpa. It's fun because my grandma plays games with me. I love my small family.

Lang, 11, China

c

3 James's blog ♪ ♪ ✕

I live in the United States. Our house is big. We have a very big kitchen and there are four bathrooms in the house. We have three washing machines for all the dirty clothes.

My friends have small families but I have a mom and dad, six sisters, and nine brothers. Big families are great! In my family, the big children help the small children. My sister, Jill, is seventeen and she helps me with my homework and music practice. She's bossy but she's nice, too.

James, 12, United States

4 Ask and answer.

1 How big is your family?
2 Are families in your country big or small?

YOUR TURN!

Think and write.

	Good	Bad
Small family	more time with parents	no brothers or sisters to play with
Big family		

3 Circle T = True or F = False.

1 James likes his big family. T / F
2 Lang is happy. T / F
3 Lang plays games with her sisters. T / F
4 In the United Kingdom, all families are small. T / F
5 Kyle likes his new brothers. T / F

1 A:25 **Listen and read. Who is hard-working? Who is lazy?**

1 After school, Maddy meets her friends.

Go away, Kipper!

2 In the afternoon, Emma and Dan do their homework. Maddy and Robbie play computer games.

You should do your homework first.

I know. Go away, Kipper!

3 After dinner, Maddy brushes her teeth. But she can't go to bed!

Go away, Kipper!

4 You must do your homework now.

5 Before bed, Maddy does her homework.

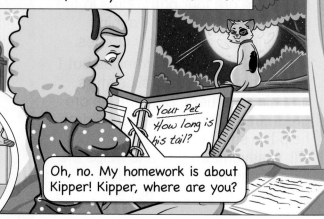

Your Pet How long is his tail?

Oh, no. My homework is about Kipper! Kipper, where are you?

2 A:26 **Listen and say.**

a
brush my teeth

b
make my bed

c
wash my face

d
clean my room

e
do my homework

f
meet my friends

g
study before a test

h
take notes in class

i
take out the garbage

j
be on time

3 A:27 **Work with a friend. Listen and play the memory game.**

Daily activities

4 Listen and number. Then say.
What must Emma do before bed?

You must brush your teeth. *(Order)*

You should brush your teeth. *(Advice)*

She must take out the garbage.

5 Unscramble and write. Then say. What is Mom saying?

1 shower / you / bed / must / before

_____

2 teeth / after meals / you / brush / must / your

_____

3 room / must / clean / you / your / every day

_____

4 homework / your / must / you / do / now

_____

You must shower before bed.

6 Look and match. Then say. What advice can you give Maddy?

Sorry, I'm late.

I have a test on Monday.

I'm bored.

I don't have class notes.

a take notes in class

c be on time

b meet her friends

d study before a test

She should be on time.

7 (A:30) **Listen and say.**

		Monday	Tuesday	Wednesday	Thursday	Friday
a	never					
b	sometimes					
c	usually					
d	often					
e	always					

8 (A:31-32) **Listen to the song and write.**

SONG

I _____ wash my face before school.

But I _____ brush my hair so I look cool.

I _____ make my bed,

And I _____ help my mom.

But I never, never clean my room.

I never, never clean my room.

My brother _____ his room.

My sister cleans her room.

My friends clean their rooms,

But not me! Oh, no! Not me!

I never, never clean my room.

I never, never clean my room.

Where's my sister's kite? Is it under the bed?

And on the chair what's that? A monster's head!

My brother's ball is here, too.

But where is it? Well, I don't know.

Because I never, never clean my room.

I never, never clean my room.

Never, never clean my room.

9 **Look at Activity 8 and write.**

1 He _____ makes his bed.

2 He _____ washes his face before school.

3 He _____ brushes his hair.

4 He _____ cleans his room.

10   **Look at the table and say.**

She always brushes her teeth.

A:33 **LOOK!**

I never brush my teeth.
He sometimes brushes his teeth.
She usually brushes her teeth.
They often brush their teeth.
We always brush our teeth.

Sasha's week	Monday	Tuesday	Wednesday	Thursday	Friday
brushes her teeth					
makes her bed					
does her homework					
meets her friends					
cleans her room					

11 **Check (✓) to complete the table about yourself. Then write and tell a friend.**

My week	Monday	Tuesday	Wednesday	Thursday	Friday
brush my teeth					
make my bed					
do my homework					
clean my room					
take out the garbage					

I sometimes take out the garbage.

1 _____

2 _____

3 _____

4 _____

5 _____

12  **Read and circle. What's your score?**

QUIZ! ARE YOU A MORNING PERSON?

Some people like mornings. What about you?

1 Do you get up on time in the morning?
1 No, never.
2 Yes, sometimes.
3 Yes, usually.
4 Yes, often.
5 Yes, always.

2 Do you have a big breakfast?
1 No, never.
2 Yes, sometimes.
3 Yes, usually.
4 Yes, often.
5 Yes, always.

3 Do you talk to your friends and family before school?
1 No, never.
2 Yes, sometimes.
3 Yes, usually.
4 Yes, often.
5 Yes, always.

4 Do you make your bed in the morning?
1 No, never.
2 Yes, sometimes.
3 Yes, usually.
4 Yes, often.
5 Yes, always.

5 Do you make your family's breakfast?
1 No, never.
2 Yes, sometimes.
3 Yes, usually.
4 Yes, often.
5 Yes, always.

6 Do you get to school on time?
1 No, never.
2 Yes, sometimes.
3 Yes, usually.
4 Yes, often.
5 Yes, always.

YOUR SCORE!

6–14 You're not a morning person. You shouldn't do important things before lunch!

15–22 You're OK in the morning but not great.

23–30 Wow, you're a morning person. You should do everything in the morning!

13 **Look at Activity 12 and talk about your day.**

I usually get up on time in the morning.

TIP!
should + not = shouldn't

14 A:34 **Listen and circle T = True or F = False.**

1 Emma is a morning person.   T / F

2 Emma always makes her bed in the morning.   T / F

3 Emma never has a big breakfast.   T / F

4 Emma sometimes helps in the kitchen.   T / F

5 Emma usually doesn't like talking in the morning.   T / F

6 Emma often doesn't get to school on time.   T / F

15 **Read. Is Jonas healthy?** (A:35)

Jonas is a soccer player. He must practice every day and he often meets his friends for a game of tennis, too. His energy comes from his food. Pasta is his favorite! He's very healthy because he eats meat, vegetables, cereals, and fruit. His bones and teeth are strong because he likes drinking milk. Jonas always brushes his teeth after meals and again before bed, and he always goes to the dentist for a check-up in March and September.

HEALTHY MENU FOR TUESDAY

★ BREAKFAST ★
Cereal with milk
Toast
A banana
Orange juice

LUNCH
Chicken pasta with green salad
An orange
Water

DINNER
Vegetable soup and bread
Fish, potatoes, and carrots
Apple pie
Milk

16 **Say.**

1 Jonas likes playing soccer and ….
2 Jonas's favorite food is ….
3 After meals, he always ….
4 Jonas likes drinking ….

17 **Write.**

1 Apples and oranges are examples of this. _____

2 This is a white drink. It makes bones and teeth strong. _____

3 This is a drink made from fruit. _____

4 To keep your teeth healthy you should sometimes visit this place. _____

5 This is an orange vegetable. _____

THINK!

What kinds of foods are bad for your teeth? Why?

Plan a menu with three healthy meals. Share it with your family and try it at home.

A:36 **Listen and read.**

STORY

19 **Why do the thieves want the Captain's map? Discuss your answers.**

Consolidation

20   **Circle T = True or F = False.**

1 Captain Formosa never gets up at eight. T / F

2 He sometimes reads his map. T / F

3 The map is a treasure map. T / F

4 The map is not in the box. T / F

5 Penn is a penguin. T / F

6 The penguins are escaping. T / F

21   **Role-play the story.**

22 **What do you give to friends and family?**
Write *never*, *sometimes*, *usually*, *often*, or *always*.
Then share with a friend.

Giving is great.

What do you do?	You	Your friend
1 Give birthday cards.		
2 Give small birthday gifts.		
3 Share music.		
4 Send text messages.		
5 Give tickets for a show.		
6 Invite friends to play.		

Do you give birthday cards?

Yes, I always give birthday cards.

HOME-SCHOOL LINK

Make a card to give to someone in your family.

PARENT

24 **A:37** **Listen and circle.**

1 He (always / never) brushes his teeth and washes his face.

2 My train never comes (on time / late).

3 She (never / usually) makes her bed in the morning.

4 He (usually / often) goes to bed late.

5 She (never / often) meets her friends.

6 Tomorrow, the students (must / should) give the mini-project to the teacher.

7 He (shouldn't / doesn't) eat chocolate every day, and he (never / should) go to see a dentist.

8 He (sometimes / usually) gets up at six and goes to school (early / on time).

---

25 **Unscramble and write. Then number.**

a kite / is / this / Matt's

_____ ☐

b garbage / the / I / out / always / take

_____ ☐

c go / late / to / you / bed / shouldn't

_____ ☐

d clean / room / should / your / you

_____ ☐

e can't / friends / I / meet / my

_____ ☐

> 1 Your friends are coming this afternoon.
> 2 No, it isn't. It's his sister's.
> 3 I like helping at home.
> 4 I must do my homework.
> 5 You must get enough sleep.

 I can talk about daily habits and give friendly advice. ☐

I can talk about how often I do things. ☐  **TEACHER**

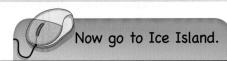 Now go to Ice Island.

Review Units 1 and 2

1 Read, look, and number.

1 My brother is seven. He has curly, brown hair and gray eyes. He's very funny but he's lazy.

2 My mom has long, light hair and blue eyes. She's sporty. She plays tennis every day. She's talkative and sometimes bossy.

3 My teacher isn't very tall. She has long, straight hair. She's a good teacher because she's clever and always very kind.

4 My friend is in my class at school. He's short and has blond hair and glasses.

Amy

a Fergus

b Mrs. Taylor

c Ben

d Mrs. Picton

2 Ask and answer.

A: What does Amy's teacher look like?

B: She has long, straight hair.

A: What's Amy's teacher like?

B: She's clever and kind.

3 Ask and answer.

1 What must you do in the morning?

2 What should you do after school?

3 What must you do before bed?

4 What should you do every day?

I must make my bed in the morning.

4 **Read and say. Then listen and check your answers.**

my   his   her   our   their

In the evening, ….

1 I sometimes   (meet / friends)
2 Fergus and Ben always (do / homework)
3 Fergus never   (clean / room)
4 Mom often   (wash / hair)
5 I usually   (make / bed)
6 Ben and I always   (brush / teeth)

> In the evening, I sometimes meet my friends.

5 **Write three sentences.**

> My dad never takes out the garbage and he never sets the table for dinner.

1 _____

_____

2 _____

_____

3 _____

_____

I   mom/dad
sister/brother
he   she   they

always
sometimes
never

but

and

do my homework
clean the bathroom
take out the garbage

set the table for dinner
go to bed before me
get dressed before breakfast

1 A:39 **Listen and read. Is Robbie good at throwing?**

2 A:40 **Listen and say.**

1 hitting

2 kicking

3 throwing

4 catching

5 diving

6 going shopping

7 telling jokes

8 reading poetry

9 trampolining

3 A:41 **Listen and number using the words in Activity 2.**

a ☐   b ☐   c ☐   d ☐   e ☐   f ☐   g ☐   h ☐   i ☐

LOOK!

What's he/she good at?	He's/She's good at hitting.
What are they good at?	They're good at hitting.
He/She isn't good at catching. / They aren't good at catching.	
What does he/she like/love doing?	He/She likes/loves going shopping.

4 A:43 **Stick. Then listen and number.**

Number 1. What's she good at?

She's good at diving.

5 **Look at Activity 4. Ask and answer.**

6  **Listen and say.**

VOCABULARY

a playing video games

b playing chess

c playing the drums

d acting

e singing in a choir

f running races

g singing karaoke

h in-line skating

7 **Listen to the song and write.**

SONG

Chorus:

Come and have fun at the Fun Club! Come here and meet new friends.

_____, trampolining, _____.
At the Fun Club, the fun never ends.

What do you like doing?

Do you like playing the _____, or _____?
There's fun for everyone.

What are you good at? Are you good at playing _____?

We love Fun Club. It's fun here! Yes! Yes! Yes!

(Chorus)

8 **Ask and answer.**

A: What are you good at?
B: I'm good at telling jokes.
A: What do you like doing?
B: I love trampolining but I don't like running races.

LOOK!

A:47

What were you doing yesterday at 7:00?	I was going to school.
What was he/she doing yesterday at 7:00?	He/She was going to school.
What were they doing yesterday at 7:00?	They were going to school.
Were you going to school?	Yes, I was. / No, I wasn't.
Was he/she going to school?	Yes, he/she was. / No, he/she wasn't.
Were they going to school?	Yes, they were. / No, they weren't.

9 A:48 **Listen and circle. Then ask and answer.**

P.M.	Robbie	Emma	Maddy and Dan
2:45	studying English	playing volleyball	reading in the classroom
	singing in music class	trampolining	drawing pictures
5:00	playing chess at school	shopping	doing their homework
	reading comic books	playing video games	acting

What was Robbie doing yesterday at 2:45?

He was studying English.

10 A:49 **Listen and match. Then ask and answer.**

11:00 reading in class   10:00 in-line skating   7:00 walking to school

11:00 making a project   12:00 having lunch

7:00 sleeping

 **1**   **2**   **3**

10:00 swimming

12:00 having lunch

12:00 having lunch   11:00 playing chess

7:00 having breakfast   10:00 writing a story

What was Robbie doing yesterday at 7:00?

He was ....

11 **A:50** **Listen and match.**

Laura   Antonio   Fred

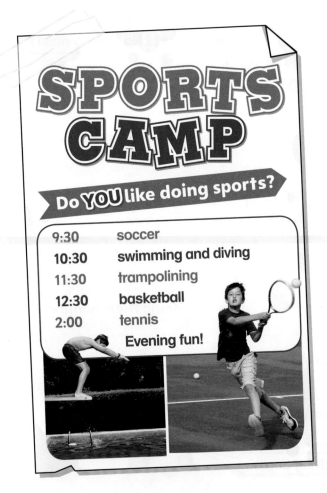

SPORTS CAMP

Do YOU like doing sports?

9:30	soccer
10:30	swimming and diving
11:30	trampolining
12:30	basketball
2:00	tennis
	Evening fun!

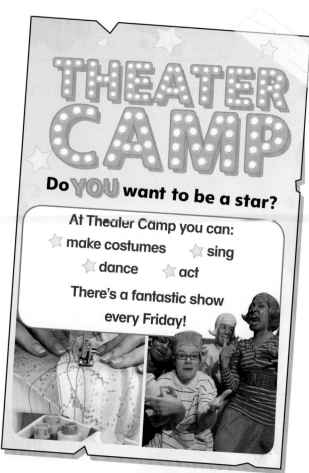

THEATER CAMP

Do YOU want to be a star?

At Theater Camp you can:

⭐ make costumes   ⭐ sing

⭐ dance   ⭐ act

There's a fantastic show every Friday!

12  **A:50** **Listen again and circle T = True or F = False.**

1 Laura is good at hitting balls.   T / F

2 Laura can dance.   T / F

3 Antonio loves playing soccer.   T / F

4 Antonio is good at throwing and catching.   T / F

5 Fred likes swimming.   T / F

6 Fred is good at singing.   T / F

13 **Look and choose. Tell a friend.**

> I like Sports Camp because I love diving and I'm good at playing tennis.

14 **Read. Then write T = True or F = False.**

This is Harry Gregson-Williams. He writes music for movies and computer games.

What movies is your music in?
The Shrek movies, the Narnia movies, and a lot of others.

You write music for computer games, too. Do you like playing computer games?
Computer games are OK but they aren't my favorite thing. I write my music on computers so I don't like playing on computers when I'm at home.

What instruments can you play?
I'm good at playing the piano and I can play the drums. I'm good at singing, too.

What's your favorite music?
Oh ... I can't answer that question. I love listening to violins and trumpets but I love a lot of music!

HE'S IN FOR THE ROYAL TREATMENT

DREAMWORKS
SHREK THE **THIRD**

1 He's good at playing the piano.   _____
2 He can't sing.   _____
3 He likes violin music.   _____
4 He writes the stories for movies.   _____
5 He loves playing computer games.   _____

15 **Correct the false sentences in Activity 14. Say.**

16 **Listen to the music and number.**

a violins ☐

b drums ☐

c piano ☐

d trumpet ☐

THINK!

Circle below. Good interview questions are:
short / long
polite / rude

MINI-PROJECT

Write five questions for a "How musical are you?" interview. Then ask a friend.

17 **Listen and read.**

1. Where's Finn?

He's watching polar bears.

Polar bears?!

2. Be careful! Polar bears can be dangerous.

3. Hey, Dylan. Can polar bears stand up?

Yes, they can and they can run!

4. Are they good at climbing?

5. And do they like reading?

Reading?

Hey! They have the map!

6. Finn! They aren't polar bears!

I know! It's the thieves!

7. Wait!

I can't stop!

TTHHHWUMPP!!!!

8. 8.5?

9!

18 Why do the penguins think of numbers? Discuss your answers.

42 Consolidation

19 **Circle T = True or F = False.**

1 Polar bears can't stand up.   T / F

2 Polar bears can be dangerous.   T / F

3 Finn was watching from behind the mountain.   T / F

4 The thieves were reading a comic book.   T / F

5 Finn falls off the mountain.   T / F

6 The thieves have the map.   T / F

20 **Role-play the story.**

21 **Check (✓) what you want to try.**

VALUES

Try new things.
Have a hobby.

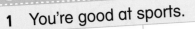

1 You're good at sports.

Take dancing lessons.

Join a sports team.

Learn martial arts.

2 You're good at drawing and painting.

Take an art class.

Learn to draw comic strips.

Learn to make jewelry.

3 You're good at singing and acting.

Learn to play an instrument.

Join the school drama club.

Start a band with friends.

I'm good at technology.

4 You're good at technology.

Learn computer programming.

Learn to make video games.

Build a website.

You should learn computer programming.

HOME-SCHOOL LINK

Try a new activity with your family.   **PARENT**

22 Follow the lines. Find and unscramble the letters. Then write.

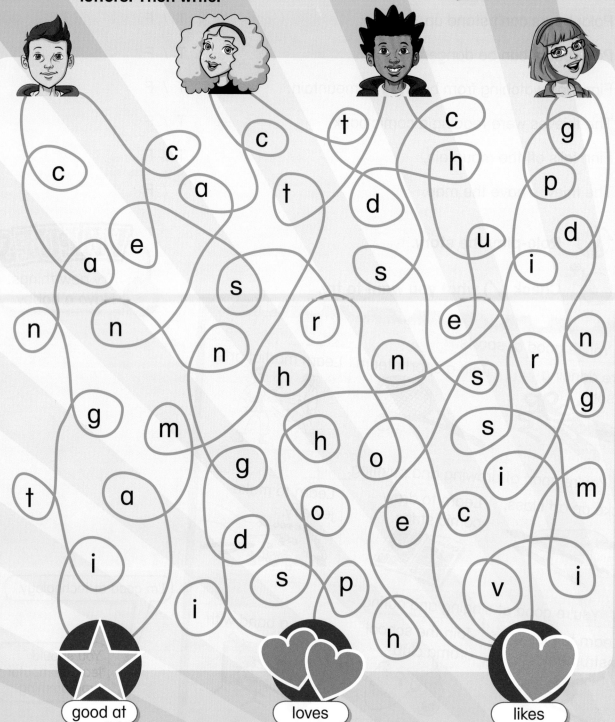

good at

loves

likes

1 Robbie _is good at acting_. He _____, too.

2 Maddy _____. She _____ playing _____, too.

3 Dan _____. He _____, too.

4 Emma _____. She _____, too.

23 **Listen and check (✓).**

What were they doing yesterday?

1 Emma	2 Dan	3 Maddy	4 Mom and Dad
a ☐	**a** ☐	**a** ☐	**a** ☐
b ☐	**b** ☐	**b** ☐	**b** ☐
c ☐	**c** ☐	**c** ☐	**c** ☐

24 **Unscramble and write questions. Then write the answers.**

1 Emma / playing / was / chess

_____

2 the / drums / was / playing / Emma

_____

3 singing / was / in / a / Dan / choir

_____

4 were / shopping / Mom / and / Dad

_____

5 comic / Mom / were / and / reading / Dad / books

_____

_____

I CAN

I can talk about things I'm good at and love. ☐

I can talk about what I was doing yesterday. ☐

 TEACHER

 Now go to Ice Island.

Wider world 2
Funny sports

1 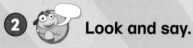 Listen and read. What are the people doing?

2 Look and say.

It's elephant polo!

a This is a ball sport.
b This is a sport with food.
c This is a winter sport.
d People ride in this sport.
e People run in this sport.

1

Mud racing

Hi. I live in Scottsdale, Arizona, in the United States. In my town, there's a mud race every year. It's for children only. They can run, climb, swim, and dive in mud. It's really funny. That's my brother in the photo. He loves mud!

Bianca, 11, United States

2

Cheese rolling

Every May, people roll a big cheese down Cooper's Hill here in the United Kingdom. Then everyone runs down the hill. They want to catch the cheese. The winner can eat the cheese. My dad likes doing the race but he never wins. He isn't very good at running!

Freddy, 11, United Kingdom

③ Reindeer racing

People love doing this sport in winter here in Tromso, Norway. The people don't ride the reindeer. They go on skis. The races are in the streets of the town and everyone shouts for their favorite reindeer. I love watching reindeer racing.

Ingrid, 11, Norway

④ Elephant polo

People usually play polo on horses but, here in India, people sometimes play polo on elephants. They sit on elephants and hit the ball with very long sticks. I don't play because I'm not good at hitting the ball. But I like watching.

Rajeev, 12, India

3 **Read again and choose. Tell a friend.**

A: I want to do cheese rolling.

B: Why?

A: Because I'm good at running and I love eating cheese!

YOUR TURN!

Think and write.

In my country, people love ....

1 **A:56** **Listen and read. Does Dan like crocodiles?**

Dan: Look! There's a competition for a round-the-world trip. The winner goes to the United Kingdom, Egypt, and China, then Australia and Brazil.

Maddy: Wow, there are a lot of interesting places you can see in the United Kingdom. In Egypt there are the Pyramids, and in China there's the Great Wall.

Dan: Sounds great! And in Brazil and Australia there are some beautiful beaches.

Maddy: But, mmm, Dan ... there are crocodiles, sharks, and big spiders in Australia, too.

Dan: What?!

Maddy: Don't worry. There are a lot of children in this competition. There's little chance of winning!

2 **A:57** **Listen and say.**

ⓐ
China

ⓑ
Korea

ⓒ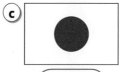
Japan

ⓓ
Australia

ⓔ
the United States

ⓕ
Mexico

ⓖ
Colombia

ⓗ
Brazil

ⓘ
Argentina

ⓙ
the United Kingdom

ⓚ
Spain

ⓛ
Italy

ⓜ
Egypt

ⓝ
India

3 **In which continent is your country?**

Asia   Australia   North America   South America   Europe   Africa

4 (A:59) **Listen and write ✓ = There are or ✗ = There aren't. Then say.**

WILD VACATIONS

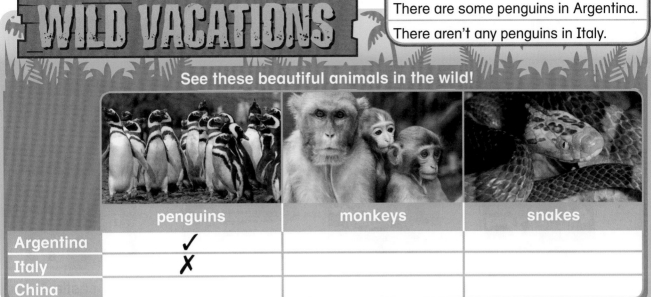

See these beautiful animals in the wild!

	penguins	monkeys	snakes
Argentina	✓		
Italy	✗		
China			

There are some penguins in Argentina.

5 **Play the game.**

A: There aren't any penguins. There aren't any monkeys. There are some snakes.

B: It's Italy!

6 **Look and say.**

monkey   dog   people   boat   rocks   shark
in the sea   in the tree   on the beach

There's a dog on the beach. There aren't any people in the tree.

7 **Listen and say.**

pyramid

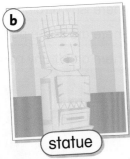
statue

cave

volcano

city

town

farm

factory

castle

TIP!
factories
cities
volcanoes

SONG

8 **Listen to the song and write.**

Chorus:

The drums are calling.
My home is calling.
I want to be there—in _____!

Tell me about your country!
I can tell you a lot.
Is there a _____?
Yes, there is. It's hot, hot, hot!

(Chorus)

Are there any _____?
Yes, there are … and there are lakes,
_____, forests, and mountains.
It's a beautiful place!

(Chorus)

Are there any old _____?
Yes, there are. It's true.
With wonderful big _____,
And _____, too.

(Chorus)

What things are there in Mexico?

There's a desert in Mexico.

9 **Look at Activity 8. Ask and answer.**

Is there a pyramid in the city?	Yes, there is. / No, there isn't.
Are there any beaches in Australia?	Yes, there are some beautiful beaches in Australia.
Are there any volcanoes in the United Kingdom?	No, there aren't.

10 A:64 **Listen and number. Then ask and answer.**

Is there a volcano in the city?

No, there isn't.

11 **Ask and answer about your country.**

A: Are there any deserts?

B: No, there aren't.

12 Read. What is the name of the statue?

Dear Archie,
Hello from Egypt! It's very hot here but it's fun.
This postcard is from Giza. In the desert at Giza,
there are some big pyramids and there's a big
statue, too. It's called the Sphinx. It has a man's
head and a lion's body. It's very, very old. From
Giza, you can see the city of Cairo.
Our hotel is on an island in the River Nile. There
aren't any cars on the island. Everyone goes by
boat. I can see some big white birds in the river.
This round-the-world trip is fantastic! Are there
any fun lessons at school this week?
See you soon!
Mia

Archie Joseph
103 Park Street
Denver, CO 80216
United States

PAR AVION

 13 Circle T = True or F = False.

1 There are some big pyramids in the desert.   T / F

2 The Sphinx is a very old statue.   T / F

3 The Sphinx has a lion's head.   T / F

4 Mia's hotel is on an island.   T / F

5 There are some hippos in the river.   T / F

 14 Talk about where Mia can travel in your country.

A: Mia can go to Whitesea Island.

B: Why?

A: Because there are some good beaches
and there's a pretty waterfall, too.

B: OK. Let's choose Whitesea Island.

Read. Does Inuk like summer or winter?

i-Blog Home | My favorites | Pictures | Log out

My recent pictures   Click here to read more

Hi. I'm Inuk.
I live in Greenland.
Winter and summer are
very different here.

My recent blogs

Winter

In the winter, we don't see the sun very much. There's one long night for four weeks in December and January. There are some big snowstorms and it is very, very cold. We go to school by snowmobile because we can't use a car.

Summer

In the summer, there aren't any snowstorms. There are often long sunny days. For a month, it is never nighttime! I go kayaking and fishing every day. The summer is great but it's very short. In September, it's time for my winter clothes again.

 Read again and say _summer_ or _winter_.

1 People use boats.
2 People use snowmobiles.
3 There are very long days.
4 There are big snowstorms.
5 There isn't very much sun.

THINK!

There aren't any deserts, rain forests, or volcanoes. There are penguins but there aren't any polar bears. There isn't any sunlight for six months every year. Where is it?

 Choose a place you want to live in and tell a friend.

A: I want to live there because I love playing in the snow.
B: I don't want to live there. I love the sun.

MINI-**PROJECT** Write about summer and winter in your country.

A:67 **Listen and read.**

STORY

1. Captain, the thieves have the map but can you remember it?

2. Yes! There's a forest ....

And there's a statue.

3.

4. And there's a pyramid.

A pyramid? There aren't any pyramids on Ice Island.

5. No, sorry. That's a different map.

Wait! I remember! The treasure is in a cave!

A cave? Are there any caves on the island?

6. Oh, no! Snow again!

Hey, snow .... Snow Mountain! There's a cave on Snow Mountain!

19 **Does Captain Formosa have maps of other places? Discuss your answers.**

20  **Write.**

1 The thieves have the _____.

2 The treasure is in a _____.

3 There aren't any _____ on Ice Island.

4 There's a _____ and a _____ on the map.

5 There's a _____ on Snow Mountain.

6 You can eat _____ and chips at the Old Harbor Inn.

21 **Role-play the story.**

22 **Check (✓) the pictures where people work in a team.**

VALUES
Teamwork is important.

23 **Write three things that can only be done in a team. Tell the class.**

1 _____

2 _____

3 _____

HOME-SCHOOL LINK
Tell your family why teamwork is important.

 PARENT

24 Look at the pictures and circle the words in the puzzle.

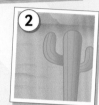

M	C	D	E	S	E	R	T	X	C	A	V	E	K
E	M	W	V	T	V	G	Q	N	O	L	P	E	W
X	B	N	F	A	R	M	M	J	L	Y	T	B	R
I	V	C	X	T	Z	G	X	K	O	R	E	A	Z
C	M	S	D	U	F	G	H	J	M	K	L	Q	C
O	X	C	V	E	B	P	Y	T	B	R	C	W	H
N	J	M	S	D	F	G	H	J	I	K	I	L	I
Q	A	U	S	T	R	A	L	I	A	W	T	R	N
T	P	Y	P	Z	X	C	V	B	N	M	Y	S	A
D	A	F	V	O	L	C	A	N	O	G	H	J	K
Z	N	C	V	B	N	M	Q	W	R	T	Y	P	L

25 Unscramble the words and find the secret message.

a There are pyramids and deserts.

EXOMCI ⬚ ⬚ ⬚ ⬚ ⬚ ⬚₆

b There's a very large rain forest.

RIZBAL ⬚ ⬚₁₁ ⬚₉ ⬚ ⬚₁₂ ⬚₁

c There are pandas and snakes.

NAICH ⬚ ⬚ ⬚ ⬚₈ ⬚

d There are beaches but there aren't any pyramids.

AASUTRIAL ⬚ ⬚₄ ⬚₁₀ ⬚ ⬚ ⬚ ⬚ ⬚ ⬚

e There's a very long river.

TEYGP ⬚₂ ⬚₅ ⬚ ⬚₁₃ ⬚

f There are castles and farms but there aren't any deserts.

TEH NEUDIT NIGDKMO ⬚ ⬚ ⬚ ⬚ ⬚ ⬚₃ ⬚ ⬚ ⬚ ⬚ ⬚ ⬚ ⬚ ⬚₇ ⬚ ⬚

Secret Message = ⬚₁ ⬚₂ ⬚₃ ' ⬚₄ ⬚₅ ⬚₆ ⬚₇ ⬚₈ ⬚₉ ⬚₁₀ ⬚₁₁ ⬚₁₂ ⬚₁₃

26 Listen and check (✓) or write.

1 ⓐ  ⓑ

2 ⓐ  ⓑ

3 ⓐ  ⓑ

4 ⓐ  ⓑ

5 ⓐ  ⓑ

6 ⓐ  ⓑ

7 There are _____ and _____ in Mexico.

8 There are _____ _____ in Colombia.

9 There are _____ _____ in Australia, but there isn't a _____.

10 There's a _____ in China, but there isn't a _____.

I CAN
I can talk about countries and places. ☐
I can answer questions about my country. ☐

 TEACHER

 Now go to Ice Island.

Review Units 3 and 4

1  Write.

> helping   sunny   watching
> good at   like   answering

Hi again. Do you remember me? I'm Amy. Last weekend I was ¹_____ at my school's Open Day. I was showing people the school and ²_____ their questions. I ³_____ doing this type of thing.

I'm Amy's teacher. Last weekend was good weather. It was ⁴_____. I was ⁵_____ Amy and the other students. They were ⁶_____ their jobs. I love seeing my students helping the school.

2 (A:69) Listen and write.

1 What was Amy's mom doing?

_____

Is she good at it? _____

Does she like it? _____

2

What was Amy's brother doing?

_____

What does he like doing? _____

Is he good at it? _____

3 What was Amy's friend doing?

_____

Does he love doing it? _____

Is he good at it? _____

3 🖊 **Write the country name.**

1 The flag of this country is yellow, blue, and red. _____

2 This country is in Europe. It has a red and yellow flag. _____

3 In this big Asian country there are many big cities and
there is a very long wall. _____

4 This country is an island. It has a red and white flag. _____

5 There are many mountains and volcanoes in this country.
It is next to the United States. _____

6 There are many large lakes in this big country in South America.
It has a blue, white, and yellow flag. _____

4 🖊 **Think about your town or city. Check (✓) the true sentences.
Then ask and answer.**

1 There are some lakes. ☐

2 There are some beaches. ☐

3 There are some farms. ☐

4 There is a harbor. ☐

5 There is a volcano. ☐

6 There are some caves. ☐

7 There are some factories. ☐

Are there any lakes?

Yes, there are.

5 🖊 **Write about your country.**

In my country there are _____.

_____

_____

_____

_____

_____

1 B:02 **Listen and read. Does Emma buy the jacket?**

1. How much is that scarf?

It's six dollars and fifty cents.

2. And how much are those sunglasses?

They're fifteen dollars.

3. Wow! I love that jacket, and it's only twelve dollars.

4. May I buy the jacket, please?

$124.00

Yes, of course. One hundred and twenty-four dollars, please.

What?!

2 B:03 **Listen and say.**

 a jacket

 b swimsuit

 c watch

 d bracelet

 e wallet

 f handbag

 g umbrella

 h gloves

 i sunglasses

3 **Look and say. Use words from Activity 2.**

I like that blue jacket.

4 B:05 **Listen and stick. Then ask and answer.**

B:04 **LOOK!**

How much is this/that jacket?	It's ninety dollars and fifty cents.
How much are these/those sunglasses?	They're thirty dollars.

a

b

c

d

f

g

e

i

h

Stick

How much is that handbag?

It's fifty-nine dollars and fifty cents.

5 **Look and imagine prices. Then role-play the conversation.**

A: How much is that pen?
B: It's three dollars and fifty cents.
A: May I buy it, please?

a pen

b candy

c guitar

d drum set

e computer

f T-shirt

g scarf

h sandals

6 (B:06) **Listen and say.**

tight

baggy

c

cheap

d

expensive

e

old-fashioned

f

modern

7 (B:07-08) **Listen to the song and write.**

TIP!
That jacket is too tight. Those sunglasses are too expensive.

8 **Look and say.**

sunglasses / big
socks / baggy
scarf / long
jacket / tight
pants / short

Her sunglasses are too big.

SONG

That jacket's too _____.
And the color's too _____.
That hat's too _____.
    And the size isn't right.

Chorus:
I only like wearing …
Baggy pants, baggy pants, baggy pants, baggy pants.
Baggy pants are _____, baggy pants are cool.
Baggy pants rule!

That sweatshirt's too _____.
Those shorts are too _____.
Those gloves are too _____.
    And the color is wrong.

(Chorus)

62 **Presentation**   *Adjectives to describe clothing and accessories*

9 **B:10** **Listen and match.**
Then ask and answer.

B:09 **LOOK!**

Whose watch is this?		Whose pens are these?	
It's	Maddy's. mine. yours. his. hers.	They're	Dan's. mine. yours. his. hers.

5

1

a

2

b

c

3

4

d

Whose sunglasses are these?

They're Robbie's.

10 **Look at Activity 9 and write.**

1 The jacket is _____Dan's_____. It's _____Dan's_____ jacket. It's _____his_____.

2 The sunglasses are _____. They're _____ sunglasses.
They're _____.

3 The bracelet _____.
_____

4 The swimsuit _____.
_____

11 **Read. Are these stories, ads, or emails?**

CRAZY CLOTHING™ Are your clothes too small, too old, or too boring?

COME TO

CRAZY CLOTHING!

We have a lot of clothes for boys and girls.
Beach clothes, sports clothes, school clothes.

They're all here at CRAZY CLOTHING!

24 LONG STREET, RIVERSIDE

Very Cool SPORTS

ARE YOU LOOKING FOR NEW SPORTS CLOTHES?
ARE THE SPORTS STORES IN YOUR TOWN TOO EXPENSIVE?

We have thousands of soccer shoes, sneakers, swimsuits, shorts, T-shirts, and gloves for men, women, and children.

Visit our website!

RIVERSIDE MARKET

Shopping is fun at Riverside Market.
Saturdays and Sundays, 9.30–5.30

- Clothes from around the world
  - Meat
  - Cheese
  - Games
- Fruit
- Toys
- Books

12  **Write.**

1 Where can you buy toys?

_____

2 Where is Crazy Clothing?

_____

3 Where can you buy cheap sneakers?

_____

4 Can you buy food at Riverside Market on Sunday?

_____

5 Can you buy gloves at Very Cool Sports?

_____

6 Can a man buy his clothes at Crazy Clothing?

_____

13 (B:12) **Read. Then number.**

Choose the right shoes!

We all love wearing our favorite sneakers. But for some activities, sneakers aren't a good idea. Find out how to choose the right shoes.

a

b

c

1  In good weather, sneakers are great for walking in a city. But on a rainy day, your feet get wet. Sneakers are too soft for walking in the mountains. They can be dangerous. Always wear stiff walking shoes or boots.

3  For rock climbing, you want to feel the rock with your feet. Sneakers are too big for this. Climbing shoes are small and tight.

2 Dancers move and bend their feet a lot. The sneakers in this picture are good for dancers because the soles are soft in the middle. The soles of other sneakers are too stiff.

What shoes do you wear for your favorite sport?

---

14 **Read again and say** *walking*, *rock climbing*, **or** *dancing*.

1 You can't wear shoes with hard soles.
2 Your feet bend a lot.
3 The right shoes are very tight.
4 Soft shoes can be dangerous.

THINK!

You want to spend a weekend camping in a cold, mountainous place. What shoes and clothes should you take with you? Make a list.

15 **Talk about the activities.**

A: I don't like rock climbing because it's too dangerous.
B: Really? I love rock climbing!

 MINI-**PROJECT** Design some sneakers. Show the class and talk about them.

 **Listen and read.**

STORY

Snow Mountain is very cold.

1

Ooh! Can I buy those gloves, please?

2

Argh! Ow! It's too tight!

3

You're too fat!

No! You're too thin!

4

Hey! The thieves!

Where's the map?

5

Quick! Run!

Stop!

6

Hey! Come back!

  Why is Jenny buying gloves? Discuss your answers.

18   **Circle T = True or F = False.**

1 Snow Mountain is always warm.   T / F

2 The thieves are in the living room.   T / F

3 One thief is too fat.   T / F

4 The thieves still have the map.   T / F

5 Jenny is buying some gloves.   T / F

6 The thieves walk to the boat.   T / F

19 **Role-play the story.**

20 **Look and stick. Then discuss with a friend. Compare your choices.**

VALUES

Dress correctly for each occasion.

A lunchtime beach party in summer

Dinner with older family members.

School graduation ceremony.

①

②

③

Stick

HOME-SCHOOL LINK

Plan an outfit for an event that you are going to.

PARENT

Comprehension / Values   *Dressing suitably for particular occasions*   **67**

21 Play the game.

How to play

Start at the top and follow the lines until you get to the bottom. Change direction when you get to another line. You can only go down, right, or left, never up! Match the names at the top with the items at the bottom.

Maddy	Robbie	Dan	Emma

jacket	watch	gloves	umbrella

HAVE FUN!

Whose jacket is it?

It's _____.

Whose watch is it?

It's _____.

Whose umbrella is it?

It's _____.

22 Play again and say. You can add extra lines to change the game. Add your own names for Number 4.

1

Maddy	Robbie	Dan	Emma

guitar	pants	computer	sunglasses

2

Maddy	Robbie	Dan	Emma

book	sneakers	toy	socks

3

scarf	sandals	T-shirt	shoes

$1	$5	$10	$15

How much is that scarf?

It's ten dollars.

Whose gold is it?

It's mine!

4

$10	$100	$1,000	gold

23  **Listen and check (✓).**

1

2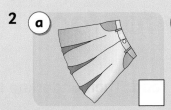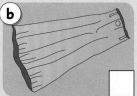

3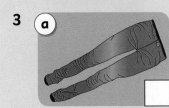

4

5

6

7

8

24  **Write.**

1 **Maddy:** _____ pens are these?

2 **Robbie:** They're not mine. Are _____ Emma's?

3 **Maddy:** No, they're not _____. Maybe they're Dan's?
Hey, Dan. Are these _____ pens?

4 **Dan:** Let's see … Ah, yes, this black pen is _____, thanks. But the red pen isn't mine.

5 **Maddy:** Well, whose pen is it?

6 **Robbie:** I don't know. Let's ask Mr. Smith. I think it's _____.

 **I CAN**
I can talk about how much things cost. ☐
I can talk about who things belong to. ☐

 TEACHER

 Now go to Ice Island.

Wider world 3
Shopping for food

1 🔘 **B:15** **Listen and read. Then underline the foods.**

1 Bao's blog ✕

In Vietnam, we buy our food at the floating market. It opens at four o'clock in the morning. There are a lot of boats and you can climb from one boat to another to buy things. You can buy fish, rice, coconuts, bananas, … and snakes, too! Some of the snakes can dance. I love watching them. Some people buy snakes for dinner but I don't eat snakes—they're too expensive.

Bao, 12, Vietnam

2 Silvia's blog ✕

In Buenos Aires, Argentina, there are some amazing bakeries. You can buy a lot of different types of pastries there. There's a lot of *dulce de leche* or milk caramel in the pastries. I often go to a bakery after school with my friends. Pastries are my favorite food.

Silvia, 11, Argentina

3 Lily's blog ✕

I live in the United Kingdom. Some families, like mine, don't buy fruit at the supermarket. We grow it in our garden. It's too cold for peaches and bananas, but we have a big plum tree and two apple trees in the garden. In spring and summer, we grow vegetables, too. There are some hens in the garden and we eat their eggs. There's only one problem—they love eating our vegetable seeds!

Lily, 12, United Kingdom

2 **Circle.**

1 The floating market opens in the (morning / evening).

2 You can buy (snakes / cakes) at the floating market.

3 Silvia (always / often) goes to a bakery after school.

4 In the summer, Lily's family grows (flowers / vegetables).

5 Lily gets her fruit from the (garden / supermarket).

3 **Ask and answer.**

1 Where does your family buy food?

2 Are there any markets in your town? What do they sell?

3 Do you grow any food in your garden?

YOUR TURN!

Think and write.

My favorite place to buy food is ....

Party time

1 (B:16) **Listen and read. Why is there a cake?**

2 (B:17) **Listen and say.**

make/made

have/had

come/came

give/gave

get/got

sing/sang

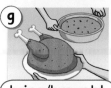
bring/brought

meet/met

eat/ate

see/saw

3 **Read and say. Use words from Activity 2.**

The family   Mom   Maddy   Maddy's aunts

The family gave Grandpa presents.

Irregular past tense verbs

4 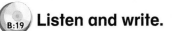 **Listen and write.**

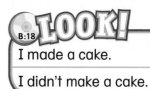 **LOOK!**
I made a cake.
I didn't make a cake.

This is a photo of your Aunt Susan's birthday forty years ago. She was eleven and we
1 _____ a small party at home. Those are her friends, Robert and Tracey. They
2 _____ her a great present and we 3 _____ her a bicycle—she really
4 _____ a lot of presents! The girl with me is your mom. She was only five then.
Those good-looking young people are your grandma and me. Yes, we
were only thirty-five! Your grandma 5 _____ a big chocolate
cake. And that baby in her arms is your Uncle David. He
6 _____ a lot of cake that day. What a mess!

Grandparents (35)

Uncle David (1) Aunt Susan (11)

Robert and Tracey (10)

Mom (5)

5 **Look at Activity 4 and say.**

1 Susan's family …. (have)   2 Aunt Susan …. (get)

3 Robert and Tracey …. (bring)   4 Maddy's grandparents …. (give)

5 Maddy's grandma …. (make)   6 Uncle David …. (eat)

Susan's family
had a party.

6 **Look at Activity 4. Play True or False.**

the family   Susan   Susan's friends   Maddy's Mom
the baby   a doll   pizza   strawberry cake

A: The baby didn't eat chocolate cake.

B: False! The baby ate chocolate cake.

7 (B:20) **Listen and say.**

1st first
2nd second
3rd third
4th fourth
5th fifth
6th sixth
7th seventh
8th eighth

9th ninth
10th tenth
11th eleventh
12th twelfth
13th thirteenth
14th fourteenth
15th fifteenth

16th sixteenth
17th seventeenth
18th eighteenth
19th nineteenth
20th twentieth
21st twenty-first

8 (B:21-22) **Listen to the song and write.**

SONG

It was the _____ of December, snowy and white.

I _____ to a party that cold winter's night.

We danced, _____,
_____, and had fun.

There were games. There were drinks for everyone.

Then ... 10, 9, 8, 7, 6, 5, 4, 3, 2, 1 ...
It was 12 o'clock! Another new year!

We said _____ to the old year.

We said _____ to the new.

My friends, new and old, said,
"Happy New Year!"

"Happy New Year!" I said, too.

9 (B:23) **Listen, repeat, and say the next date.**

a February 22nd
b April 14th
c November 1st
d July 31st
e September 19th

> February twenty-second,
> February twenty-third

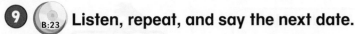

B:24 LOOK!

Where did you go?	I went to Ghana.
When did you go to Ghana?	I went on August 1st.
What did you see?	I saw giant butterflies.

6

10 **B:25** **Read. Then listen and write the dates.**

This diary belongs to: Jenny Powell

August

1st — I went to Ghana and met my relatives from Africa for the first time.

_____ — I went to Kakum National Park and saw beautiful giant butterflies.

_____ — I went to a soccer game in Accra. Ghanaians love soccer! I danced and sang soccer songs with my new friends.

10th — I went to the north of Ghana. I saw the giant baobab trees and ate some baobab fruit, but I didn't like it!

_____ — I went to Lake Volta and sailed in a pirogue, a type of boat. It was cool!

_____ — We had a party. My African friends gave me a lot of presents. "Come back soon!" they said. I cried at the airport. ☹

_____ — I came back home! I brought lots of presents for my mom, dad, and brother. It was a great experience!

11 **Look at Activity 10. Ask and answer.**

1 She …. (meet)
2 She …. (see)
3 She …. (dance)
4 She …. (sing)
5 She …. (eat)
6 She …. (have)
7 She …. (come)
8 She …. (bring)

When did she go to Ghana?

She went on August 1st.

12 (B:26) **Read. Was yesterday fun for Harry?**

Sally's Welcome party

Who? Sally's friends, classmates, and teachers

Where? Hope School

When? Saturday, April 18th

What time? 6.30–9.00 p.m.

Harry's blog

Sunday, April 19th

Yesterday, we had a welcome party for Sally, a new student at school. Before the party, I went to my friend Mark's house for pizza. Then we went to school together in his dad's car. We saw all our friends there. Sally's parents were there, too. There was cool music but the room was too hot. We talked and played games. Then there was a dancing competition. A lot of the girls were good at dancing and Mark was good, too. He and Sally got a prize! We had a lot of fun!

13  **Circle.**

1 The party was at (school / Mark's house).

2 Harry met Mark (before / after) the party.

3 The party was on (Saturday / Sunday).

4 There was good (food / music) at the party but the room was too (hot / cold).

5 The children (talked / ate), played, and danced.

6 (Mark / Harry) and Sally got a prize.

14 **Imagine you are Mark. Talk about the party.**

> Harry was at my house before the party.

15 B:27 **Listen and read. Then stick.**

1 In the fall of 1620, 102 settlers went from England to North America. Their ship's name was the *Mayflower*. The settlers' first winter in North America was very cold and snowy. They didn't have any food. The settlers were hungry and scared.

2 In the spring, some Native Americans went to see the settlers. "We can help you," they said. "We are good at fishing and farming."

3 The Native Americans taught the settlers about growing food in their country. In the fall, the settlers said, "We have a lot of food now."

4 The settlers and Native Americans had a special dinner and party. They ate a big meal and the settlers said thank you to the Native Americans for all their help. This was the first Thanksgiving.

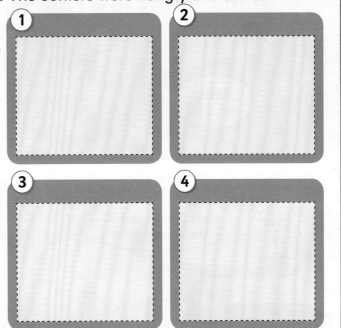

① ② ③ ④

Stick

16 **Circle T = True or F = False. Then correct the false statements.**

1 The *Mayflower* was a ship.   T / F

2 The settlers were from North America.   T / F

3 Their first months in North America were fun.   T / F

4 The Native Americans were good farmers.   T / F

5 The Native Americans taught the settlers to cook.   T / F

6 There was a lot of food at the first Thanksgiving. T / F

THINK!

What and how much food and drink should you get for a summer evening party with 20 friends?

17 **Play *Who said it?***

1 "We can help you."

2 "Thank you."

3 "We are good at fishing and farming."

4 "We have a lot of food now."

A: "We can help you."

B: The Native Americans said, "We can help you."

MINI-
PROJECT

Find out the history of a celebration in your country. Write about it.

18 B:28 **Listen and read.**

19 **How can they get into the cave? Discuss your answers.**

20   **Circle T = True or F = False.**

1 The thieves don't have the map.   T / F

2 The thieves went into a store.   T / F

3 Captain Formosa was on his submarine.   T / F

4 The entrance to the cave is near a statue.   T / F

5 The thieves went to the cave in a snowmobile.   T / F

6 The penguins are in the snowmobile.   T / F

21 **Role-play the story.**

22 **How good are you at solving problems? Talk about a solution for each problem.**

VALUES
Be a creative problem solver.

Problem 1:
You don't know the meaning of a word.

Problem 2:
You wrote your project and want to check your spelling.

Problem 3:
You want to make friends at school, but you are shy.

I don't know the meaning of this word. What should I do?

You could look it up in a dictionary.

HOME-SCHOOL LINK

Tell a family member about a problem you solved at school. **PARENT**

23 Can you read the messages? Write.

HAVE FUN!

CODE 1 DZ GXF X QAK MXLSC

1	2	3	4	5	6	7	8	9	10	11	12	13	14	15	16	17	18	19	20	21	22	23	24	25	26
A	B	C	D	E	F	G	H	I	J	K	L	M	N	O	P	Q	R	S	T	U	V	W	X	Y	Z
																					O				

Example: the twenty-second letter is really the fifteenth ➜ code letter V = O

The fourth letter is really the twenty-third.	The sixth letter is really the fourth.	The thirteenth letter is really the sixteenth.
The last letter is really the fifth.	The seventeenth letter is really the second.	The twelfth letter is really the eighteenth.
The seventh letter is really the eighth.	The first letter is really the ninth.	The nineteenth letter is really the twentieth.
The twenty-fourth letter is really the first.	The eleventh letter is really the seventh.	The third letter is really the twenty-fifth.

Message 1 =

CODE 2 XF BUF B MPU PG DBLF

1	2	3	4	5	6	7	8	9	10	11	12	13	14	15	16	17	18	19	20	21	22	23	24	25	26
A	B	C	D	E	F	G	H	I	J	K	L	M	N	O	P	Q	R	S	T	U	V	W	X	Y	Z

The second letter is the first.	The third letter is the second.	The fourth letter is the third, and so on.

Message 2 =

24 Make your own code. Write a message to a friend.

1	2	3	4	5	6	7	8	9	10	11	12	13	14	15	16	17	18	19	20	21	22	23	24	25	26
A	B	C	D	E	F	G	H	I	J	K	L	M	N	O	P	Q	R	S	T	U	V	W	X	Y	Z

Code

Message

25 B:29 Listen and number.

26 B:30 Read. Then write.

I play basketball. My team is called Yellow Birds. On Saturday it was the last game of the season. Before the game my team had 94 points and were second in the league. Brown Bears were first. But because we won our last game we went to first on 97 points. Brown Bears were second on 96 points. Blue Ducks were fourth before the last game on Saturday. They beat Red Cats so they went up to third on 80 points. Red Cats went down from fourth to fifth and ended with 78 points. Green Tigers were last in the league with only 70 points because they lost to Silver Snakes on Saturday. Silver Snakes went up to fourth on 79 points.

	TEAM NAME	POINTS	POSITION
a	Red Cats	78	
b	Green Tigers		
c	Brown Bears	96	2nd
d	Silver Snakes		
e	Yellow Birds		
f	Blue Ducks		

I CAN

I can use irregular past tense verbs. ☐

I can use ordinal numbers. ☐

TEACHER

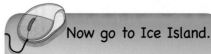
Now go to Ice Island.

Review Units 5 and 6

1 Choose a present. Write the letter. Then ask and answer.

Whose scarf is this?

It's Uncle Andy's.

1 My grandparents often go to hot places.

2 My baby cousin, Ollie, likes animals.

3 Aunt Caroline loves baggy clothes.

4 My parents love sports and they love playing video games.

5 Uncle Andy often goes to cold places. He likes skiing.

a $____.____

b $____.____

c $____.____

d $____.____

e $____.____

2 (B:31) Order the sentences. Then listen to the dialogue and check your answers.

a Shop clerk: Yes, of course. Eighteen dollars and fifty cents, please. ☐

b Shop clerk: They're eighteen dollars and fifty cents, please. ☐

c Dan: May I buy the pants, please? ☐

d Dan: How much are those baggy pants? ☐

3 Write prices for all the items in Activity 1. Then role-play using the dialogue in Activity 2.

4  Say.

Kathryn went to the United Kingdom on January tenth.

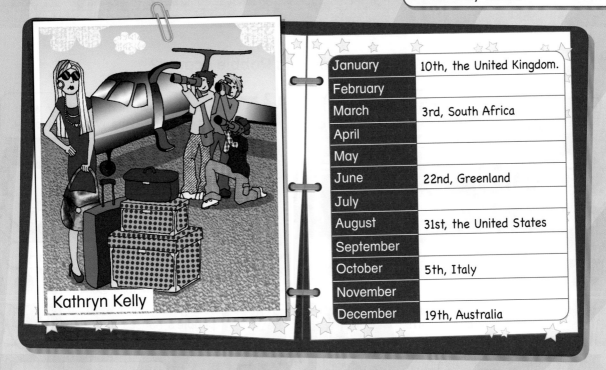

Kathryn Kelly

January	10th, the United Kingdom.
February	
March	3rd, South Africa
April	
May	
June	22nd, Greenland
July	
August	31st, the United States
September	
October	5th, Italy
November	
December	19th, Australia

5  Say.

1 What did Kathryn do?
2 What was the problem?

In the United Kingdom, she used many taxis. The problem was she wanted to walk but the evenings were too dark.

the United Kingdom / evenings / dark

the United States / horse / small

Australia / sun / hot

6 Write.

1 My sister _____ my lunch to me yesterday. (bring)

2 I _____ to the store and _____ many clothes last week. (go / see)

3 I _____ my friends in the city yesterday. (meet)

4 We _____ karaoke at school two days ago. (sing)

1 B:32 **Listen and read. Why are Emma and Robbie scared?**

1

There was a story writing competition at school today.

Did you win?

No, I didn't. My story wasn't very good. Writing a good story is difficult!

2

Dan was the winner. His story was about a green hand without a body.

Was it scary?

Of course it was scary! The green hand went to people's houses and ....

3

Argh!

4

Ha-ha! Good joke, Dan!

Dan! That wasn't funny!

2 B:33 **Listen and say.**

a  interesting

b boring

c exciting

d  scary

e  funny

f difficult

g easy

h  romantic

3 **Talk about these things. Use words from Activity 2.**

Talking with friends is interesting.

skateboarding   vacations   dark nights   talking with friends
swimming   math class   reading newspapers   sci-fi movies
reading comic books   playing the piano

LOOK!

Was it interesting?	Yes, it was. / No, it wasn't.
Was there an alien in it?	Yes, there was. / No, there wasn't.
Were there any exciting stories?	Yes, there were. / No, there weren't.

4 B:35 **Listen and write ✓ or ✗.**

Story competition winners!

① ISLAND ADVENTURE by James Duncan

② MIKE GOES TO MARS by Isabella Brand

③ Nile Princess by Vinny da Souza

	①	②	③
exciting?	✓	✗	✓
scary?			
funny?	✗		✗
children?	✓	✓	
an alien?		✓	✗

5 **Look at Activity 4. Ask and answer.**

Was "Mike Goes to Mars" exciting?

No, it wasn't.

6 **Look at Activity 4. Play the guessing game.**

A: Was it exciting?
B: Yes, it was.
A: Were there any children in it?
B: Yes, there were.
A: It was "Island Adventure!"

7 B:36 **Listen and say.**

a computer science

b math

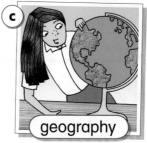
c geography

d science

e history

f art

g music

h P.E.

8 B:37-38 **Listen to the song and write.**

SONG

Chorus:
Math, _____, history, _____, art,
_____.
A lot of subjects every day. Is school boring? No way!

Last year, _____ wasn't easy. The lessons weren't always fun.
But now I can do all my homework. Math is for everyone!

(Chorus)

Last year, _____ was boring. P.E. lessons weren't my thing.
But now it's my favorite subject. I can play soccer and swim.

(Chorus)

9 **Look at Activity 8 and write. Then say.**

Last year, math wasn't easy.

Jill

		Math	P.E.
Jill	last year		
	this year		
You	last year		
	this year		

LOOK! B:39

Did you have computer science on Tuesday?	Yes, I did. / No, I didn't.
Was math difficult?	Yes, it was. / No, it wasn't. It was easy.

10 B:40 **Listen and circle or write. Then ask and answer.**

	Monday	Tuesday	Wednesday	Thursday	Friday
Robbie	math	music	geography	English	history and art
	easy / difficult	easy / difficult	interesting / boring	easy / difficult	easy / difficult
Emma	_____	science	_____	computer science	_____
	difficult	_____	boring	interesting	_____

Did Robbie have music on Tuesday?

Was it easy?

Yes, he did.

No, it wasn't.

 11 B:41 **Read. Then listen and write.**

1 Did Maddy have math homework on Monday? _____

Was it easy? _____

2 Did she have art homework on Wednesday this week? _____

Was it boring? _____

3 How about on Friday? What was her homework on Friday?

_____

Was it difficult? _____

12 **Read. Then number.**

We love . . .

SCHOOL TRIPS!

Where did you go on your last school trip?

1 Our science trip yesterday was exciting but scary, too. We went to a cave. In some places, there weren't any lights and the cave was very dark. There were lots of bats. Yuck! Bats are awake at night. They sleep inside the cave during the day and go out to eat at night.

Sam, 10, Seoul, Korea

2 Last fall, my class went on a history trip to the center of my city. We were learning about life 400 years ago and looking at very important buildings around a square. Our teacher said, "Take lots of photos, draw pictures, and write about the buildings." It was a fun day.

Luisa, 10, Lima, Peru

3 On Thursday, I wasn't at school. I went on a geography trip to a lake in the hills. The river in my city starts at this lake. We went to a waterfall on the river, too. It wasn't very big but it was really beautiful. We learned that the water here is clean.

Oliver, 11, Leeds, United Kingdom

13 **Say *True* or *False*. Correct the false sentences.**

1 Luisa went on a geography trip last fall.

2 Luisa learned about life 200 years ago.

3 Oliver and his class were in a city.

4 There was a beautiful waterfall on the river.

5 Sam's science trip was boring.

6 There weren't any animals in the cave.

> False. She didn't go on a geography trip. She went on a history trip.

14 **Look at Activity 12. Talk about the trips.**

> Luisa's trip was interesting. I like old places.

15 (B:43) **Read. Who were Tara's friends?**

Star Interview!

Tara, 11

Tara, 14

Tara, today

A lot of people know about your life as a movie star in Hollywood. But where was your home when you were a child?
In the middle of the desert in Australia. It was 200 kilometers from other children and 500 kilometers from a city!

Was it very boring?
No, it wasn't. It was interesting. There were horses on our farm and we also had a pet kangaroo. The animals were my friends.

Where was your school?
I didn't have lessons at school. My teacher was on a radio in the city and I was on a radio at home. There were other students on the radio, too, and every year there was a big party in the city. I was shy with the other children but it was always a very exciting day.

16 **Ask and answer.**

1 Was Tara's first home in Hollywood?
2 Were there any animals on her farm?
3 Were her lessons in the city?
4 Was there a teacher?
5 Was there a party every month?
6 Were the parties exciting?

THINK!

You want to make a project about your grandpa's or grandma's school life. Write four questions to ask when you interview them.

17  **Imagine you live in Tara's first home. Ask and answer.**

1 Is your life interesting?
2 Who are your friends?
3 What do you do every day?
4 Do you like your lessons? Why? / Why not?

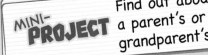
MINI-PROJECT Find out about a parent's or grandparent's school.

18 Listen and read.

1

Here's the statue.

But where's the cave?

2

I can't see it! It isn't here.

Come on, Dylan. You're good at geography. Where's the cave?

3

Heeeeelp!

4

The cave's here.

5

Ooooh! That was scary!

No, it wasn't. It was exciting!

Be careful, kids ....

6

Look, the thieves! And the treasure!

7

Ha-ha-ha! I have the treasure!

We! We have the treasure.

We're too late!

  19 Why can't they find the cave at first? Discuss your answers.

90 Consolidation

20 **Circle T = True or F = False.**

1 Dylan is good at geography.   T / F

2 There aren't any statues.   T / F

3 Finn is in a tree looking for the thieves.   T / F

4 Finn falls into the cave.   T / F

5 Dylan said, "That was scary!"   T / F

6 The kids got the treasure.   T / F

21 **Role-play the story.**

22 **How much do you know about what your older family members were like when they were younger? Take the test. Then ask and answer.**

VALUES

Learn about your older family members' youth.

Family member	I know! (score 2 points)	Score
1 For my _____,	school was (fun / boring).	
2 For my _____,	math (was / wasn't) easy.	
3 My _____	(was / wasn't) good at sports.	
4 My _____	(loved / hated) romantic movies.	
5 My _____	enjoyed (scary / funny) movies.	
6 My _____'s	favorite food was _____.	
7 My _____'s	favorite drink was _____.	
8 My _____'s	favorite movie star was _____.	
9 My _____'s	favorite singer/band was _____.	
My total score		/ 18

18–15 Very good! You know a lot. 14–10 Good! You know some things. 8–0 You should learn more. Find out when you get home today.

HOME-SCHOOL LINK

For my mom, school was fun.

Find out some other things about what your older family members were like when they were younger.

PARENT

23 Find and circle the school subjects. The letters that are left tell you the answer!

G	E	O	G	R	A	P	H	Y
C	O	M	P	U	T	E	R	I
L	S	C	I	E	N	C	E	I
M	A	T	H	K	E	M	U	S
S	C	I	E	N	C	E	I	C
A	N	H	I	S	T	O	R	Y
A	R	T	D	M	U	S	I	C
S	C	I	P	E	E	N	C	E

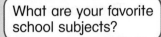

What are your favorite school subjects?

24 Find and circle the adjectives. The letters that are left tell you the answer!

How about Tom? What is his favorite subject?

T	O	I	G	M
F	U	N	N	Y
B	L	T	I	R
O	D	E	T	A
R	I	R	I	C
I	F	E	C	S
N	F	S	X	I
G	I	T	E	K
E	C	I	E	S
E	U	N	A	N
G	L	G	S	L
I	T	S	Y	H

25 (B:45) **Listen and write.**

	Monday	Tuesday	Wednesday	Thursday	Friday
1st class	🧪	📚 ABC		📚 ABC	
2nd class	English	🧪	1 + × % / 2 − ÷ √	1 + × % / 2 − ÷ √	
3rd class	1 + × % / 2 − ÷ √	1 + × % / 2 − ÷ √	🌐		1 + × % / 2 − ÷ √
LUNCH					
4th class	🌐		🎨	🎵	🎨
5th class				🏀	

26 ✏️ **Unscramble and write questions. Then match.**

1 go / did / in / you / cave / the

_____

2 bats / any / there / were

_____

3 boring / was / it / trip / a

_____

4 boat / was / a / there

_____

5 go / any / did / places / you / other / to

_____

a Yes, there were. It was exciting!

b No, it was interesting.

c Yes, we went to a lake near the cave.

d No, there wasn't.

e Yes, we did. It was dark and wet.

I CAN
I can use adjectives to describe things in the past.
I can talk about school subjects in the past tense.

☐
☐

 TEACHER

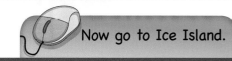 Now go to Ice Island.

Wider world 4
Unusual schools

  Listen and read. Then number.

1
Kai's blog

My new school in Tokyo is great. It's international so I have friends from forty different countries! They always speak to me in English—their English is great. I'm learning Japanese. It was difficult at first but my friends were kind when I said the wrong words. Now it's easy.

Kai, 12, Japan

2
Abi's blog

I love my school! I go to a special school in the mountains. Students go there to study winter sports. Every day, after studying geography, math, and other subjects, we do sports for three hours. We go skiing and snowboarding. Some students from our school went to the Olympics. I want to be a famous skier, too.

Abi, 14, Canada

c

Matu's blog ✕

I live in my school because it's a boarding school. My friends and I all live in rooms next to the school. I love living with my friends and the teachers are all very nice. In the evening, there are a lot of activities. We can watch movies or go swimming but usually we have homework.

Matu, 12, Kenya

4  **What is important about school for you? Tell a friend.**

- good friends
- a swimming pool
- good teachers
- a lot of sports
- students from other countries

> A swimming pool is important for me because I like swimming.

2 **Ask and answer.**

1 Who lives in a school?
2 Who is learning Japanese?
3 Who does sport for three hours a day?
4 Who has friends from forty countries?

3 **Ask and answer.**

1 Which school in Activity 1 do you want to go to?
2 What do you like about your school?

YOUR TURN!

Think and write.

subjects   sports
number of students   teachers

At my ideal school, there are science lessons every day.

1 (B:47) **Listen and read. Is Carlos playing?**

1

Where's Carlos?

2

Who's Carlos? Where's he from?

He's a famous Spanish player. He was on an American team before and on an Italian team last year. Now he plays here, but he isn't in this game.

3

Maybe he was better before.

4

CARLOS

I am a good player. But look at my leg.

It's Carlos! You're great! Sorry, my friend doesn't know anything about soccer.

2 (B:48) **Listen and say.**

a Chinese	**b** Korean	**c** Japanese	**d** Australian
e American	**f** Mexican	**g** Colombian	**h** Brazilian
i Argentinian	**j** British	**k** Spanish	**l** Italian
m Egyptian	**n** Indian		

3 **Talk about famous people from different countries.**

Johnny Depp is American.

Lionel Messi is Argentinian.

LOOK!

Is he/she from the United States?	Yes, he/she is.	No, he/she isn't.
Where's he/she from?	He's/She's from Argentina.	He's/She's Argentinian.
Where are they from?	They're from Australia.	They're Australian.

4 (B:50) **Listen and match. Then ask and answer.**

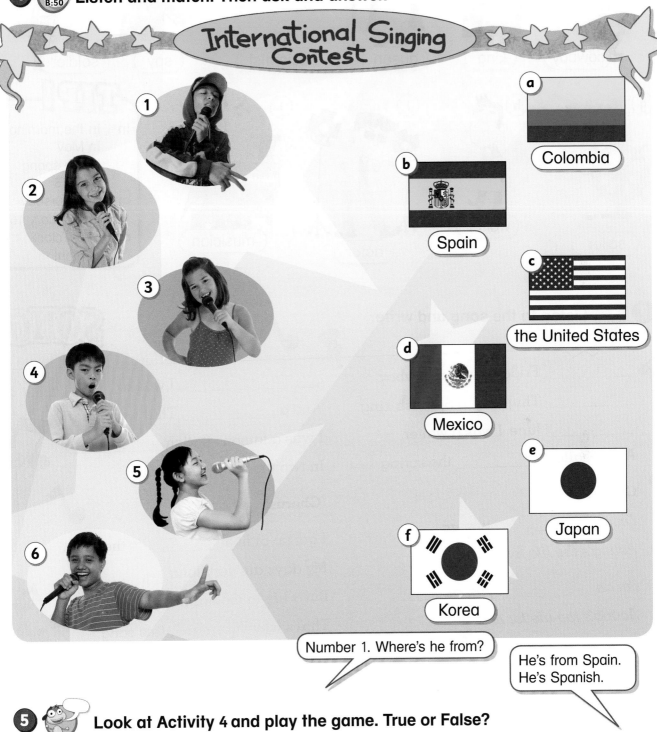

International Singing Contest

1

2

3

4

5

6

a Colombia

b Spain

c the United States

d Mexico

e Japan

f Korea

Number 1. Where's he from?

He's from Spain.
He's Spanish.

5 **Look at Activity 4 and play the game. True or False?**

A: Number 1. He's from Brazil.

B: False! He's from Spain.
He's Spanish.

A: The Colombian flag is red,
yellow, and green.

B: False! It's red, yellow, and blue.

6 B:51 **Listen and say.**

a  cowboy

b  king

c  queen

d  scientist

e  spy

f  soldier

g  sailor

h  waiter

i  actor

j musician

TIP!

in	**in** the morning
	in May
	in the spring
	in 2013
on	**on** Thursday
	on January 16th
at	**at** 5 o'clock
	at night

7 B:52-53 **Listen to the song and write.**

SONG

_____ Friday, I was a cowboy.
_____ Thursday, a Spanish king.
_____ June, I was a waiter,
And a sailor _____ the spring.

Chorus:
I'm an _____, yes, an _____.
Acting's the life for me.
I'm an _____, yes, an _____.
Acting's the life for me.

_____, I was a _____,
And a _____. That was great!
I was a famous British _____,
In two thousand and eight.

(Chorus)

I get up at five _____ the morning.
My days are very long.
But a life in movies is exciting.
That's why I'm singing this song.

(Chorus)

8 **Look at Activity 7 and say. Use in, on, or at.**

He was a waiter in June.

1 waiter / June
2 sailor / the spring
3 famous spy / 2008
4 king / Thursday
5 gets up / 5 o'clock
6 cowboy / Friday

9  **Read and write.**

1

This movie is about a Japanese scientist. She went to the Moon.

This movie is about a Japanese scientist _____ went to the moon.

She made a rocket. The rocket went to the moon.

She made a rocket _____ went to the moon.

2

This movie is about a French chef. He made cakes.

This movie is about a _____ _____ who _____ _____.

He made a wedding cake. It was very big.

He made a _____ that _____.

3

This movie is about an American waiter. He worked hard.

This movie is about _____ _____ _____.

He opened a restaurant. It was the best restaurant in New York.

He opened a _____ _____ in New York.

10 B:55 **Listen and number. Then say.**

He's the king who's eating.

11 **Play the game. Think of a famous person and give hints. Your partner guesses.**

12 **B:56** **Read. Does the writer like the programs?**

Big Kids

Channel 1 at 6:00 p.m. on Tuesday, June 28th

In this Australian program, children do their parents' jobs for a week and their parents go to school. This week, a boy is a waiter in an expensive restaurant and his dad has some problems with his math homework. Very funny!

The Finton Files

Channel 3 at 7:30 p.m. on Wednesday, June 29th

Here's an exciting spy story with interesting characters, and the actors are great! It's about Harry Finton who is an American spy in Italy 70 years ago.

Doctor Glock

Channel 5 at 10:00 a.m. on Thursday, June 30th

A scientist and his alien pet go to sea with some sailors. There are a lot of bad programs for children in the morning, but this one is fantastic!

The Big Game

Sports Channel 1 at 3:00 p.m. on Saturday, July 2nd

The Los Angeles Lakers play the Chicago Bulls in the last game of the basketball season.

13 **Write.**

Which program:

1 is on Thursday? _____

2 is funny? _____

3 is at seven thirty? _____

4 is about people a long time ago? _____

5 is in the morning? _____

6 has teams in it? _____

14 **Look at Activity 12 and choose. Tell a friend.**

> I want to watch Doctor Glock. It's exciting.

15 B:57 **Read. Then number.**

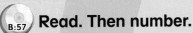

The history of video games

Every year, there are new video games. But let's look at some of the old ones ...

1 The first video games were American. Pong was new in 1972 and it was too big and expensive for people's homes. Two small white rectangles went up and down and a small white square went left and right. What was the game? Computer table tennis!

2 The Game Boy was Japanese. It was first in the stores in 1989. It was small and there were a lot of good games for it. The games were black and white. Games with the character Mario were very successful.

3 The Wii was new in 2004. In a lot of Wii games, you play with all your body and not just your fingers. Some sports games are very good exercise!

a

b

c
 PONG

16 **Ask and answer.**

1 Were the first video games Japanese?
2 Was Pong cheap?
3 Were the first Game Boy games in color?
4 Were the Mario games successful?
5 Was the Wii in stores five years ago?
6 Do you play some Wii games with your whole body?

THINK!

You can invent your own video game. What is it about?

17 **Talk about the video games that you play.**

exciting   boring   interesting   easy   difficult

Do you play Wii?

No, I don't. I think it's boring.

MINI-**PROJECT**

Ask a family member about his or her favorite childhood games.

B:58 **Listen and read.** STORY

1

Fantastic!

We're rich!

2

Aaah! A monster!

3

This is scary. What's happening?

4

Hi, kids!

It's Captain Formosa!

5

It's the Golden Penguin of Ice Island! Good job, kids!

6

Good job, penguins!

I know this statue!

It's the statue of King Penn who was my grandfather. He was king of the penguins fifty years ago.

19 **What is the treasure? Discuss your answers.**

20 **Number the sentences in the correct order.**

a The thieves' boat is on the submarine. ☐

b The thieves find the treasure. ☐

c Captain Formosa catches the thieves. ☐

d The submarine comes up under the thieves' boat. ☐

e The captain and the kids have the treasure. ☐

f The thieves are scared. ☐

g A "monster" penguin jumps out of the sea. ☐

21 **Role-play the story.**

22 **Circle and write for yourself. Then ask and answer.**

VALUES

Be a good role model for others.

A good role model is someone ….	Do you? Yes/No/Sometimes	Does your friend? Yes/No/Sometimes
1 who arrives (late / on time)		
2 who (listens / talks) more		
3 who (shares / doesn't share)		
4 who (works / doesn't work) hard at school		
5 who plays (before / after) doing homework		
6 who (helps / doesn't help) at home		
7 who (says / doesn't say) "please" and "thank you"		
8 who (thinks before doing / does before thinking)		

Do you arrive on time? — Yes, I do.

HOME-SCHOOL LINK

Tell your family how you helped your friends in class today. **PARENT**

Stick. Then play. Who did you meet?

HAVE FUN!

At 4 o'clock, I met a Mexican girl who is good at soccer.

18 Finish — Go to visit the child who is from Japan.

17 January (good at skiing)

16 Go to visit the child who is from the United States.

15 (can speak Spanish)

10 (loves singing)

11 Go to visit the child who is from Korea.

12 August (likes sailing)

13 winter (likes snowboarding)

14 Go to an English-speaking country.

9 Friday (can write Chinese)

8 Go to a country that has blue on its flag.

7 Go to visit the child who is from Mexico.

6 Saturday (likes kayaking)

5 Tuesday (can play chess)

1 Start (good at soccer)

2 April (was new at school)

3 summer (loves swimming)

4 Go to visit the child who is from Colombia.

104 Review

24  Write *that* or *who*. Then listen and circle.

1 The man _____ is selling ice cream in the park is (Italian / Spanish). The ice cream _____ he makes is great. He only comes to the park in July and August.

2 This girl is (Japanese / Korean). She usually reads after dinner at eight o'clock. The book she is reading now is (a British / an American) book. It is a funny book. The star of this book is a girl _____ can talk to monkeys!

25 Unscramble and write. Then match.

1 The man (loves / is / Australian / who / running).

_____

_____

 a

2 This woman (who / the / guitar / well / plays / very) is a Mexican musician.

_____

_____

 b

3 China is a (things / country / makes / many / that).

_____

 c

4 The United States is a (that / country / baseball / plays).

_____

_____

 d

I CAN   I can talk about where someone is from. ☐

I can use *who* and *that* to describe people and things. ☐

 TEACHER

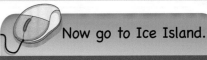 Now go to Ice Island.

Review Units 7 and 8

1 (B:60) **Listen and match. Then ask and answer.**

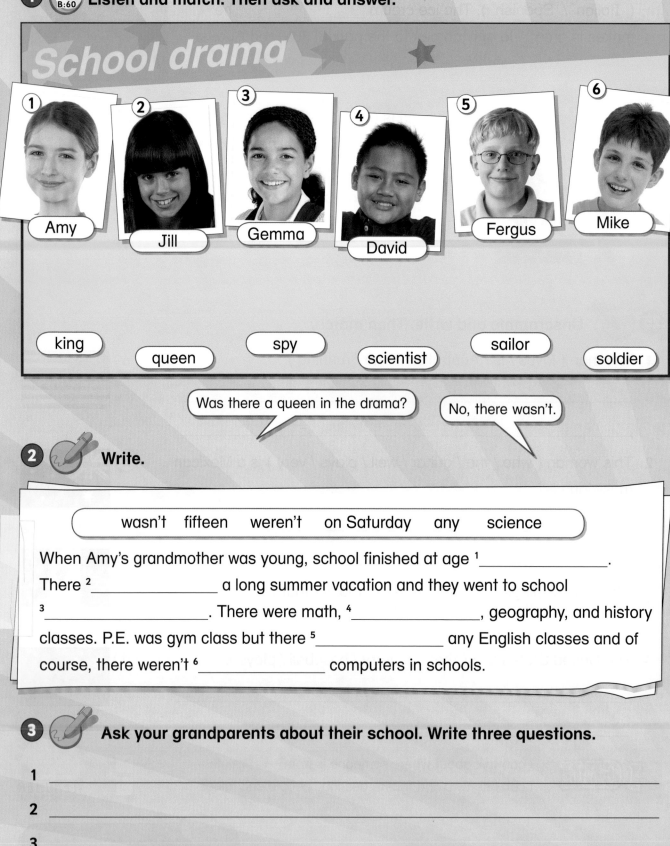

School drama

1 Amy
2 Jill
3 Gemma
4 David
5 Fergus
6 Mike

king   queen   spy   scientist   sailor   soldier

Was there a queen in the drama?   No, there wasn't.

2 **Write.**

wasn't   fifteen   weren't   on Saturday   any   science

When Amy's grandmother was young, school finished at age ¹_____.
There ²_____ a long summer vacation and they went to school
³_____. There were math, ⁴_____, geography, and history
classes. P.E. was gym class but there ⁵_____ any English classes and of
course, there weren't ⁶_____ computers in schools.

3 **Ask your grandparents about their school. Write three questions.**

1 _____

2 _____

3 _____

4 ✎ **Write.**

	Country	Nationality
1	He's from Argentina.	
2		She's Colombian.
3	They're from Italy.	
4		He's Egyptian.
5	They're from Brazil.	
6		She's Korean.
7	They're from Japan.	

5 🔊 B:61 **Listen and write. Then say.**

1 He's ___an American soldier___.

2 She's _____.

3 They were _____.

4 He's _____.

5 It's _____.

6 They're _____.

> This is a soldier who is from the United States. He wears a uniform.

> He's an American soldier.

6 ✎ **Think of animals or famous people. Write a quiz. Then ask a friend.**

1 Is Johnny Depp American? _____

2 Where are kangaroos from? _____

3 _____

4 _____

5 _____

6 _____

7 _____

Goodbye

1 B:62 **Listen and number.**

2 **Ask and answer.**

1 What was your favorite scene in the story? Why?
2 Who was your favorite character in the story? Why?
3 What was your favorite song in this book? Can you sing it?
4 Which "*Have Fun!*" page was the best in this book?

3 **Write. What unit are these pictures from?**

Unit _____   Unit _____   Unit _____   Unit _____   Unit _____

4 **Write. Who said this?**

1 "Look! He's dancing." _____

2 "Yes! There's a forest…." _____

3 "The thieves were in their boat!" _____

4 "I can't see it! It isn't here." _____

5 "He's watching polar bears." _____

5 **Write the answers.**

1 What was the name of the mountain in the story? _____

2 What's the name of the thief who is fat? _____

3 What's the name of the thief who is thin? _____

4 This is a name from the story. Who is it?
    t r n a f o a c o p s m i a _____

5 Who took the treasure map from the submarine? _____

6 Can Jenny snowboard? _____

7 What are the penguins like? _____

8 Is Dylan good at geography? _____

9 What does Dr. Al look at in the middle of the night? _____

10 What does Captain Formosa do after breakfast?

_____

6 Write. Ask a friend to read and comment.

_____ years ago I went to

_____ .

_____

_____

"I read this." Friend signs here:

_____

Friend's comment:

_____

_____

_____

7 Draw and write about your family, friends, and country. Then say.

My family

This is my _____

who is _____ .

_____ can _____ ,

but can't _____ .

_____ likes _____ .

My friends

What are they good at?

_____

What are they like?

_____

What do they look like?

_____

My country

This is _____ .

I'm _____ .

It's a country that is famous for _____

_____ .

8 Write a sentence from each unit to remind you of the language you learned in it.

Welcome Unit _____

Unit 1 _____

Unit 2 _____

Unit 3 _____

Unit 4 _____

Unit 5 _____

Unit 6 _____

Unit 7 _____

Unit 8 _____

9 **Write a country quiz. Then draw and color the flag.**

1   This is a country that _____.

2   This is a country that _____.

3   This is a country that _____.

4   This is a country that _____.

5   This is a country that _____.

10 **Write three rules for home and three rules for school. Use *must* and *should*.**

My rules

At home

1   _____
    _____

2   _____
    _____

3   _____
    _____

At school

1   _____
    _____

2   _____
    _____

3   _____
    _____

11 **Make a Golden Penguin farewell card for your friends to sign.**

First, get some paper and cut out a square.

Second, turn it over and fold Line A.

Third, fold down Line B.

Fourth, turn it over and fold Line C, and Line D.

Fifth, fold back Line E, fold back Line F, and fold down Line G.

Sixth, turn it over and draw eyes on the penguin.

It's a Golden Penguin! Good job!

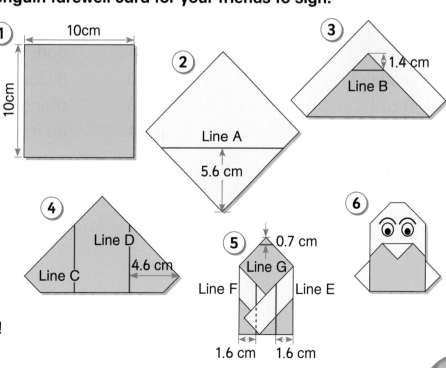

Word list

A

acting	p. 38
actor	p. 98
always	p. 26
American	p. 96
Argentina	p. 48
Argentinian	p. 96
art	p. 86
ate	p. 72
Australia	p. 48
Australian	p. 96

B

baggy	p. 62
bald	p. 12
be on time	p. 24
beautiful	p. 12
boring	p. 84
bossy	p. 14
bracelet	p. 60
Brazil	p. 48
Brazilian	p. 96
British	p. 96
brought	p. 72
brush my teeth	p. 24

C

came	p. 72
castle	p. 50
catching	p. 36
cave	p. 50
cheap	p. 62
China	p. 48
Chinese	p. 96
city	p. 50
clean my room	p. 24
clever	p. 14
Colombia	p. 48
Colombian	p. 96
computer science	p. 86
cowboy	p. 98
cute	p. 12

D

dark hair	p. 12
difficult	p. 84
diving	p. 36
do my homework	p. 24

113

Verb list

Present	Past	Past Participle
act	acted	acted
agree	agreed	agreed
be: am/is/are	was/were	been
believe	believed	believed
beat	beat	beaten
blush	blushed	blushed
borrow	borrowed	borrowed
break	broke	broken
bring	brought	brought
brush	brushed	brushed
build	built	built
burn	burned	burned
buy	bought	bought
call	called	called
catch	caught	caught
chat	chatted	chatted
check	checked	checked
choose	chose	chosen
clean	cleaned	cleaned
climb	climbed	climbed
clip	clipped	clipped

Present	Past	Past Participle
close	closed	closed
collect	collected	collected
comb	combed	combed
come	came	come
complain	complained	complained
complete	completed	completed
cost	cost	cost
count	counted	counted
cry	cried	cried
cut	cut	cut
dance	danced	danced
design	designed	designed
dig	dug	dug
do	did	done
download	downloaded	downloaded
draw	drew	drawn
dress	dressed	dressed
drink	drank	drunk
dry	dried	dried
dust	dusted	dusted
eat	ate	eaten

Present	Past	Past Participle
empty	emptied	emptied
explain	explained	explained
fail	failed	failed
fall	fell	fallen
feed	fed	fed
feel	felt	felt
find	found	found
finish	finished	finished
fix	fixed	fixed
floss	flossed	flossed
fly	flew	flown
follow	followed	followed
forget	forgot	forgotten
frown	frowned	frowned
get	got	gotten
give	gave	given
go	went	gone
hang	hung	hung
has/have	had	had
hear	heard	heard
help	helped	helped

Present	Past	Past Participle
hide	hid	hid
hit	hit	hit
install	installed	installed
join	joined	joined
jump	jumped	jumped
know	knew	known
laugh	laughed	laughed
lean	leaned	leaned
learn	learned	learned
leave	left	left
listen	listened	listened
live	lived	lived
look	looked	looked
lose	lost	lost
mail	mailed	mailed
make	made	made
meet	met	met
memorize	memorized	memorized
miss	missed	missed
mop	mopped	mopped
move	moved	moved

Present	Past	Past Participle
open	opened	opened
pack	packed	packed
paint	painted	painted
pass	passed	passed
pay	paid	paid
photograph	photographed	photographed
play	played	played
practice	practiced	practiced
prepare	prepared	prepared
print	printed	printed
pull	pulled	pulled
pump	pumped	pumped
push	pushed	pushed
put	put	put
rake	raked	raked
read	read	read
rent	rented	rented
rescue	rescued	rescued
rest	rested	rested
return	returned	returned
ride	rode	ridden

Present	Past	Past Participle
ring	rang	rung
roast	roasted	roasted
run	ran	run
say	said	said
search	searched	searched
see	saw	seen
sell	sold	sold
send	sent	sent
set	set	set
shake	shook	shaken
shoot	shot	shot
show	showed	shown
sign	signed	signed
sing	sang	sung
sit	sit	sit
skate	skated	skated
sleep	slept	slept
solve	solved	solved
stay	stayed	stayed
study	studied	studied
surf	surfed	surfed

Present	Past	Past Participle
sweat	sweated	sweated
sweep	swept	swept
swim	swam	swum
take	took	taken
talk	talked	talked
tell	told	told
text	texted	texted
think	thought	thought
throw	threw	thrown
tidy	tidied	tidied
tie	tied	tied
touch	touched	touched
trade	traded	traded
turn	turned	turned
use	used	used
visit	visited	visited
wait	waited	waited
walk	walked	walked
warm	warmed	warmed
wash	washed	washed
watch	watched	watched

Present	Past	Past Participle
water	watered	watered
wear	wore	worn
weed	weeded	weeded
whistle	whistled	whistled
win	won	won
worry	worried	worried
wrap	wrapped	wrapped
write	wrote	written
yawn	yawned	yawned
yell	yelled	yelled

Acknowledgments

The Publishers would like to thank the following teachers for their suggestions and comments on this course:

Asako Abe
JiEun Ahn
Nubia Isabel Albarracín
José Antonio Aranda Fuentes
Juritza Ardila
María del Carmen Ávila Tapia
Ernestina Baena
Marisela Bautista
Carmen Bautista
Norma Verónica Blanco
Suzette Bradford
Rose Brisbane
María Ernestina Bueno Rodríguez
María del Rosario Camargo Gómez
Maira Cantillo
Betsabé Cárdenas
María Cristina Castañeda
Carol Chen
Carrie Chen
Alice Chio
Tina Cho
Vicky Chung
Marcela Correa
Rosalinda Ponce de Leon
Betty Deng
Rhiannon Doherty
Esther Domínguez
Elizabeth Domínguez
Ren Dongmei
Gerardo Fernández
Catherine Gillis
Lois Gu
SoRa Han
Michelle He
María del Carmen Hernández
Suh Heui
Ryan Hillstead
JoJo Hong
Cindy Huang
Mie Inoue
Chiami Inoue
SoYun Jeong
Verónica Jiménez
Qi Jing
Sunshui Jing
Maiko Kainuma
YoungJin Kang

Chisato Kariya
Yoko Kato
Eriko Kawada
Sanae Kawamoto
Sarah Ker
Sheely Ker
Hyomin Kim
Lee Knight
Akiyo Kumazawa
JinJu Lee
Eunchae Lee
Jin-Yi Lee
Sharlene Liao
Yu Ya Link
Marcela Marluchi
Hilda Martínez Rosal
Alejandro Mateos Chávez
Cristina Medina Gómez
Bertha Elsi Méndez
Luz del Carmen Mercado
Ana Morales
Ana Estela Morales
Zita Morales Cruz
Shinano Murata
Junko Nishikawa
Sawako Ogawa
Ikuko Okada
Hiroko Okuno
Tomomi Owaki
Sayil Palacio Trejo
Rosa Lilia Paniagua
MiSook Park
SeonJeong Park
JoonYong Park
María Eugenia Pastrana
Silvia Santana Paulino
Dulce María Pineda
Rosalinda Ponce de León
Liliana Porras
María Elena Portugal
Yazmín Reyes
Diana Rivas Aguilar
Rosa Rivera Espinoza
Nayelli Guadalupe Rivera Martínez
Araceli Rivero Martínez
David Robin
Angélica Rodríguez

Leticia Santacruz Rodríguez
Silvia Santana Paulino
Kate Sato
Cassie Savoie
Mark Savoie
Yuki Scott
Yoshiko Shimoto
Jeehye Shin
MiYoung Song
Lisa Styles
Laura Sutton
Mayumi Tabuchi
Takako Takagi
Miriam Talonia
Yoshiko Tanaka
María Isabel Tenorio
Chioko Terui
José Francisco Trenado
Yasuko Tsujimoto
Elmer Usaguen
Hiroko Usami
Michael Valentine
José Javier Vargas
Nubia Margot Vargas
Guadalupe Vázquez
Norma Velázquez Gutiérrez
Ruth Marina Venegas
María Martha Villegas Rodríguez
Heidi Wang
Tomiko Watanabe
Jamie Wells
Susan Wu
Junko Yamaguchi
Dai Yang
Judy Yao
Yo Yo
Sally Yu
Mary Zhou
Rose Zhuang

Stickers

Unit 3 Free time   page 37

Unit 5 Shopping   page 61

$116 $15 $1,000

$29 $9.99 $30

$59.50 $20 $360

Unit 5 Shopping   page 67

Unit 6 Party time   page 77

Unit 8 Entertainment   page 104